WE LIVE IN A DANGEROUS WORLD.

Childhood is no longer idyllic. Adolescence is a far, far cry from prom night and front-porch necking. Help your children learn how to help themselves.

Have you discussed with your children what should be done if they find themselves at a questionable party? Have you ever talked about abnormal behaviour with them? Have you discussed when your child should get out of a friend's car? Does your child know when to reject adult authority? Is your child a leader? A follower? A wanderer? Do you know how much money your child spends? Have you met the parents of your child's friends?

These are just a few of the questions you should begin to ask to take positive action today—so you won't be sorry tomorrow.

A
PARENT'S
GUIDE TO
STREETPROOFING
CHILDREN

RICHARD C. GOSSAGE
&
MELVIN J. GUNTON

SEAL BOOKS
McClelland and Stewart-Bantam Limited
Toronto

A PARENT'S GUIDE TO STREETPROOFING CHILDREN
A Seal Book / March 1982

ISBN 0-7704-1709-4

Seal Books are published by McClelland and Stewart-Bantam
Limited. Its trademark, consisting of the words "Seal Books"
and the portrayal of a seal, is the property of McClelland and
Stewart-Bantam Limited, 25 Hollinger Road, Toronto, Ontario
M4B 3G2. This trademark has been duly registered in the Trade-
marks Office of Canada. The trademark, consisting of the word
"Bantam" and the portrayal of a rooster, is the property of and
is used with the consent of Bantam Books, Inc. 666 Fifth Ave-
nue, New York, New York 10103. This trademark has been duly
registered in the Trademarks Office of Canada and elsewhere.

PRINTED IN CANADA

COVER PRINTED IN U.S.A.

0 9 8 7 6 5 4 3 2 1

The authors would like to express their appreciation to all those people who took time out of their busy lives to talk about the topic of streetproofing. Special thanks to Gay Goodfellow, who provided us with invaluable research, and Diana Fisch, who produced and reproduced the manuscript quickly and cleanly. We also wish to record our deep appreciation to Anna Porter, who believed in the project, and to Jennifer Glossop, who moved the two of us into a new medium with the greatest of ease. Most importantly, we wish to acknowledge the devotion of our wives, Carol and Mary Lou, and our children, Cael, Jason, Jessica, and Patrick, who put up with us during the birth of this book.

CONTENTS

1
HELP YOURSELF

Becoming a parent is a major event in the lives of most people. The drama of the event and the helplessness of the little beings combine to make fanatics out of previously reasonable adults. When the child first comes home, caring for it becomes a major preoccupation. The problems are numerous, and the readjustments often major. But with the help of experts and support groups for everything from breast feeding to toilet training, babies and parents somehow manage to work their way through the first year together.

As two fathers going through similar experiences at the same time, we used to compare notes at work. Though one of us had two grown-up boys by a previous marriage, the personal shake-up was almost identical for both of us. One who'd been accustomed to quick weekend getaways now complained about the endless hours spent getting organized for a simple excursion. The other would describe the frustration of getting dressed up to go out, only to be hugged by a sticky-fingered child.

Though we both were aware that our children were still very fragile little beings, it soon became apparent that they were also very durable. As one year turned into two years, our energy levels began to wane. With exhaustion came a quiet acceptance of a new status quo within the family. As a result, we both became somewhat crisis-motivated. As a child reached for the wall plug, we'd purchase the plastic covers that fill the holes. As the other child staggered out of the backyard toward the street, we realized it was time for a gate to be placed in the driveway. It's not that we lacked a genuine ongoing love or concern for our babies, it's just that, like all humans, we sometimes took them for granted. Our pride in their achievements far outweighed any consideration of any serious harm that might befall them. Beyond keeping dangerous articles out of reach and locking medicine cabinets, we rarely gave serious thought to potential danger.

Our joy was so genuine that we were utterly shocked when we arrived at our office one day to be greeted by headlines about a little six-year-old girl who had been kidnapped. It's not that we'd never before heard of child tragedies. It's just that our own family happiness seemed to place this particular incident in a different perspective. As we listened to the radio that day, the drama unfolded. Apparently, the little girl had wandered away from a park near her home with a strange man. She was found that evening, brutally murdered. Shaken to the bone, we realized that it could easily have happened to our own son or daughter. Imagine the terror for the little tyke. Think of the agony of parents trying to cope with such an impossible burden. We both wondered out loud how events like this could occur. We asked ourselves if there were any way that this horror might have been prevented. A day or so later, we were both suffering from a typical middle-class reaction: "How can some parents be so negligent?" Though this righteous attitude briefly made us feel secure, it didn't last long. We thought back to our own childhoods. One of us had spent hours shooting a BB gun at a lit candle in the basement of his home. In retrospect, it was amazing that an eye hadn't been lost or the house burned down. The other had regularly played a game called Stretch. The object of this game was to make a person do the splits by throwing a hunting knife into the ground just beyond the opponent's outstretched leg. He was lucky to grow up with ten toes. As teenagers, we had both traveled in cars at speeds up to one hundred miles per hour.

The more we talked about our childhood experiences, the more apparent it became that each of us had been lucky to have survived at all. Practically every adult can add horror stories to a list like that; and while it makes for an amusing evening, it proves that relaxing as your baby turns into a child may not be the best policy.

When you think back, most healthy, happy adults have been very lucky at various times in their childhood. It's therefore fair to conclude that all children, even your own, are going to need some luck to reach adulthood safely. We wondered, however, if we couldn't provide our own kids with just a little sense of their own mortality—streetproof them—so that when they went out the door, the odds of their returning safely would be increased.

Our first inclination was to look in the bookstore. Surely there'd be some advice to help make sure they came back. There wasn't! Most authors concerned themselves with how to be a closer family, or concentrated on the difficult but possibly more interesting areas of sex and drugs.

Our next idea was to read the papers more closely. When we started to do this, we became aware that hardly a day goes by without the mention of a tragedy.

In Toronto, Ontario, a storm sewer turned into a "torrent of water" in which a thirteen-year-old boy died. Apparently, he and his friend used to bicycle regularly for about a mile down the center of a circular concrete spillway. On this particular occasion, they were met by a sudden surge of water, which engulfed them, taking the boy's life.

In Elizabeth, New Jersey, police cracked a teenage kidnap ring and charged them with abducting a ten-year-old boy and collecting a $12,000 ransom for his return. When questioned at the end of the ordeal, the youth told police that his abductors had said, "Your mother wanted us to pick you up."

In Louisville, Kentucky, an elementary school teacher was convicted of five counts of sodomy and two counts of sexual abuse for having sex with four male students.

It couldn't happen to our kids, we thought. And yet we knew it could, and the more we read, the more concerned we became about the welfare of our own children.

The field is not without experts. They're quoted extensively after every tragedy. Unfortunately, when the dust settles, it's difficult to find an organized summary of practical suggestions. As a result, we set out to create one. Instead of looking for a book on streetproofing children, we'd write one. As we saw it, streetproofing would consist of providing a child with a lot of practical suggestions and teaching him or her to rely on common sense.

The first step was to talk to the experts. We started our research with senior officers of the youth bureau of a major police force. They admitted that they spent a great deal of time dealing with kids who had real problems, but who in many ways were ordinary children just like ours. According to policemen we talked to, the basic problem is that kids like to wander. Ranging farther and farther afield is just part of growing up. It is a way of gradually separating themselves from their families. (One policeman told us that his own children liked to go to a place they described as "the danger." Obviously they recognized that the particular creek was risky, but that didn't stop them from playing there.)

They also agreed that children were maturing earlier. The average thirteen-year-old was now getting into situations that had been the exclusive preserve of seventeen-year-olds when his parents were growing up. Another change that they noticed was that kids weren't taking their friends home as much as they used to. More often, they were meeting them in plazas or other hangouts such as pinball parlours.

These statements, while they described and explained the changes and dangers, did not provide solutions. "How can we help parents help their kids *before* they get into trouble?" we asked. On this subject, the police were in complete agreement. The majority of kids who got into trouble in the street did not like themselves. The police were emphatically of the opinion that this was because they hadn't received enough attention—"positive stroking," as one of them described it. Whenever they met the parents of kids who'd run into problems, the parents were always tremendously concerned. The police wondered whether the problem might have been prevented if some of this "concern" had been turned into attention long before the crisis had occurred. They described conversations with parents who spoke of their children "growing up overnight." As they pointed out, it takes many years for a child to grow up, and if it seems like overnight, it may be because the parents just hadn't been spending enough time with their children.

There were two other points on which the police were truly eloquent and unanimous. They illustrated both by means of rather humorous stories. It seems that an officer had straightened out a youngster who had been in trouble over a minor problem. Some time after, the mother called up. "My son won't go to bed," she said. "What shall I do?" He couldn't believe his ears; the woman was asking a policeman what to do when her child wouldn't go to bed. We laughed and waited for him to make his point. It was very clear to him. Parents had forgotten that they had rights! A great number of parents were now being pushed around by their kids. We talked about it a while and agreed. Every one of us had tested our own parents at various times, but we all laughed nervously at the thought of openly defying them. That story wasn't the officer's only example. He'd seen a five-year-old youngster utterly refuse to put on his coat when asked to do so by a parent. The mother made several threats and then gave up. This was another example of a parent's failing to exercise her rights to discipline her child. She'd probably been making meaningless threats for several years. By age five, the youngster was already astute enough to recognize that he could do what he liked. His lack of respect for the adults in his immediate family had already been carried over to other adults. As the officer said, "It doesn't matter whether the threat made in the heat of the moment is somewhat unfair; it's critically important that it's followed through." After the coat incident, the parent had looked at him and said, "What can I do?"

It's a question that police are often asked, and yet the other point on which they were unanimous was that parents know what is best for their own children. It seems ludicrous to them that the people who live with a child would want advice from a policeman or policewoman whose contact with the youngster may have lasted less than a day. As they are quick to illustrate, kids have greater respect for information from their parents. With rare exceptions, the parent is the best decision maker of the bunch. They believe that if parents would simply trust their own judgment, and exercise their rights, they'd go a long way toward streetproofing their children.

Our next step was to talk to some social workers. After all, they were involved with kids and the street every day. We, of course, were aware that the social workers, like the police, were dealing with kids after they had problems. As a result, the information we received again reflected what happens to kids who have not been streetproofed successfully.

"But what can parents do about keeping their kids out of trouble?" we asked again. It seems that they didn't have direct access to material on streetproofing either. However, like the police, they had some very strong opinions. They agreed that the kids who were most likely to get into trouble on the street were those who had a low self-opinion because they felt that they were being ignored at home. One social worker described a conversation with a father whose daughter was in trouble. Though the man said that he spent a lot of time with his daughter, he could not remember when they'd last eaten a meal together. As the social worker stated, "If they dined together regularly, then maybe they'd start to talk." It's no use coming up to a child you haven't been with and saying, "So what's bugging you?" Another point on which they were emphatic was that children learn by example. One social worker provided a graphic illustration. "There's no use telling a child to go to a policeman in times of trouble, and then cursing the 'cops' in front of the child the next time you get a speeding ticket." Dealing with children, they felt, demanded some genuine sympathy. One social worker said something that hit home with both of us. She said, "All of us admit that kids' problems are just as big for them as our problems are for us, and yet few of us act in a way that indicates this to kids." For both of us it was easy to remember tears caused by a lost ball. To our youngsters that was as big a crisis in their world as a disagreement at work was in ours. And yet neither of us had shown sympathy or spent much time attempting to solve the problem.

The social workers we spoke with all believed that children who ran into difficulties often had little sense of value. If they'd had to negotiate for some of their privileges, they'd appreciate them more. The topic of conversation had circled back to parents' rights again. It was as if the effort involved in earning things when we were younger had caused us to want to give everything to our children with no strings attached. As one social worker pointed out, a kid who earns his allowance even by doing something simple around the house values the resulting privileges more and is less inclined to abuse them. In her opinion, parents have a right to expect kids to do things at home. The social workers also agreed unanimously that today's parents must follow through on what they say. One social worker dealing with a youngster on probation had said that he would double the visits if the youngster was late for a meeting without forewarning. The girl missed an appointment and was surprised to find the reporting occasions doubled. Incredulous, she said to the social worker, "You really mean what you say, don't you?" It was quite apparent that not many people had meant what they said in that particular youngster's life.

The themes tended to recur wherever we went. Teachers talked to us about the necessity of parents having a positive attitude toward their children. A prime example of lack of attention was provided by Parents' Night. Those parents who turned up were always quick to ask the same question. "So what are the problems with Johnny?" Rarely did they ask what was going right, so that they might return home and at least start by encouraging their children in those areas in which they were doing well. Teachers were also tired of being blamed for problems that had, as they said, "arrived in the classroom with the child."

When we spoke to psychologists, the conversation inevitably returned to parents. One psychologist stated that he was tired of hearing the phrase "alienated youth." He said that kids were no more or less alienated than they ever were. He felt that the phrase was used by adults who were too lazy to attempt any communication. Parents who spent time with their children did not consider them alienated. Another psychologist pointed out that kids with unhappy home lives would try to make up their deficiencies on the street. This, she said, made them more subject to peer pressure.

The more we talked to experts, the more we were told that parents, and by implication we ourselves, should know what to do with our own children. Though we'd started our investigation looking for tips on what kids should do on the street, we were continually confronted with examples of what parents should do with kids in their home. What happened in the home was clearly the greatest factor in how our youngsters would behave when they were away from us. We thought back to the newspaper clippings we'd seen. In every situation, the tragedy might have been avoided through the use of some common-sense instructions.

Our determination was to write a book on streetproofing children that was simple. We wanted to encourage parents to start relying on their common sense again, and to provide their children with advice and a sense of self-worth which the kids would take with them wherever they went. While we recognized the importance of schools, block parents, and police, we also wanted to provide tips our parents might have given. It's our hope that this book and its straightforward ideas will strike common chords for parents everywhere. Whether you choose to follow our ideas or others that occur to you while reading ours doesn't matter. The effort will have been worthwhile if the number of chilling newspaper accounts is reduced.

A Parent's Guide to Streetproofing Children is not a book of expert opinion. It is instead the combined experience and opinions of two concerned fathers who believe that the best way to help yourself is to trust yourself. If you're a parent, then you've successfully made it back to the front door of your home after a lot of trips on your own. This book will remind you of many of the things you now do intuitively— things that you should be telling your own children so that they'll come home safely, whatever their age. If they're still under your roof, it's not too late to remember.

2
KNOW YOUR NEIGHBORHOOD

If you want to streetproof your children, you are acknowledging that at least some of the dangers that concern you exist on the street. But what is a street?

If that sounds simplistic, take a moment and think about it. We did, and we came to some startling realizations.

It's easy to agree that a street is something that cars travel along. But in the sense in which we're using it, it's much broader. Really, it is anything beyond your arms, or out of your jurisdiction. It is usually, though not always, outside of the home. The street, as we're going to use the term in this book, is defined by your child's travels, and these increase every year. Your two-year-old may be limited by your property boundaries, but God knows what the limits are for your ten-year-old. That's the problem: if you're serious about streetproofing, God's knowing is not enough. Is it the schoolyard, a park, or somewhere else?

It becomes an interesting exercise to try to find out. You realize quickly that while your child's world is represented by some defined neighborhood boundaries, yours is not. As a matter of fact, your world is so large (sometimes the world itself) that you regularly pass through your child's world without noticing. Our children's world—call it a neighborhood—is often only significant to us for that brief period of time when we are choosing a place to live. Is there much traffic on the street? Has the local school a good reputation? Will the property gain in value?

15

How many of us have ever talked to people who already live in a neighborhood and have kids? It would be very useful to find out where they play and what the parents think of the area. Of course, there's no point talking to the people who are selling you the house. Quite naturally, they have a vested interest in reassuring you that you're moving into heaven.

If you're considering a new area, read the local press. It will often be a good barometer of what's happening. As a matter of fact, the local press and the local police precinct might be good places to go and have a chat. They'll quickly let you know whether there's an unpleasant place or element in your neighborhood. You should also take the time to visit some of the facilities that you have been told are there. While you may never use them, they will be very much a part of your kids' world, and you can be sure that they will be using them regularly.

Even if you are moving back into a neighborhood where you grew up, face the fact that times change. Make a thorough investigation. Adults who are living in a particular area often don't become aware of the changes until they have children. Even then, it often takes a crisis to force them into awareness.

TAKE A WALK

Once you're settled with kids in a neighborhood, your job isn't over. The first step is to find out the routes your children take to and from school and other extracurricular activities. Initially you should take, not send, your children wherever they're going. Inevitably, they have to learn to manage on their own, but it's best if you go over the territory with them first and set down some guidelines. A genuine curiosity about why your children enjoy certain places will be a great help to you. However, it's vital that you take the time to supplement this information with your own observation. If you're a jogger, you may think that you know what they're talking about. Take it from us, you don't. Even a slow jogger passes through their world far too quickly. The acid test is to spend several days taking child-speed walks around the area you live in. What's a child-speed walk? That's the pace you move at when you're not really going anywhere. It's like walking a dog that feels compelled to mark every vertical object. As a matter of fact, walking a dog is a good way of getting a child's-eye view. The same things appeal to both dogs and children. Dogs sniff at bits of paper; children pick them up. Both like to wander down blind alleys.

Just remember that dogs are creatures of routine, and children aren't. To discover your child's world, you can't always go counterclockwise around the same three blocks. Meander to just past the farthest points you've heard your youngster mention. It's an interesting experience. If you dawdle a bit, you'll suddenly notice those locations that would make great hiding places. You'll see the spaces that exist between houses and you'll discover kids playing in a construction site that you thought was fenced off. (If this happens, we hope you'll stop and find out how they got in. Whether or not you can get those children out, you should be able to prevent an accident by discussing the dangers with your child, your neighbors and, if you're smart, with the site foreman.)

Keep on walking. We learned that, instead of an unpleasant duty, we'd discovered a forgotten pleasure. Along the railway tracks we were reminded that the ties are still too close to step on every one and too far apart to jump on every other one.

PROVIDE GUIDELINES

Streetproofing is not a question of making a list of locations where your children cannot go. It is a recognition of where they might go. The challenge then is to provide guidelines that both child and adult can accept. For example, the railway walks resulted in several agreements.

Railway Tracks

First, we acknowledged that they provided an excellent short cut between our street and the neighborhood store. As a result, it could be used, *providing* the youngster agreed to remain alert for trains at all times. This meant that no catch, tag, or hide-and-seek could be played near the tracks at any time. In addition, he could not use the short cut at night because there were no lights. Finally, the tracks were out of bounds at two times: the first was in winter when hoods, scarves and ear muffs would impair hearing; the second was dictated by a schedule we obtained. When trains were due, the tracks were out of bounds.

Having arrived at these terms with our child, we walked the route, pointing out where the view was obstructed by a curve. He acknowledged the need to walk away from the tracks when he was within one hundred yards of this particular spot. Fortunately, there were no trestles, but we also discussed the dangers they would pose.

The railway example is not meant to imply that youngsters only gravitate to railway tracks, or to suggest that you shouldn't establish different guidelines for your own children. The message is that you can't just issue rules from your living room. You've just got to get into the street with your kids.

Parks and Vacant Lots

Find out where the parks and vacant lots are. Even if you think you know them, wander in and examine the equipment. Is it in good shape? If it isn't, get someone to repair it, or warn your child to stay away from it. If it's fine, you should evaluate how old a youngster should be in order to use it. A swing that is great fun for a ten-year-old may be very dangerous for a six-year-old. Explain this to your children. If they are too young, tell them which equipment is safe for them to use by themselves and which they should avoid unless accompanied by an adult. Playgrounds vary tremendously. A walk around one will give you a pretty good idea of how well it is kept. If there is a lot of litter and broken glass, then play will be dangerous and you should search for another area for your youngster.

Kids love to play in vacant lots and fields. Take a look around and see if there are any of these in your neighborhood. Though they may be exciting to kids, they're often hazardous. Many dangers, including broken glass, tin cans and dynamite, can exist. Dynamite? Well, in New York, three sticks of dynamite were found by kids in a field near a residential area. An eight-year-old girl and a little boy, whom she described as "the smartest kid on our street," saw a white cord under a bush. Her smart friend pretended he was going to throw the T.N.T. at her, but decided to take two sticks home to show his parents. While this is an extreme example, it clearly indicates that parents should warn their youngsters of the hazards posed by vacant lots and unmaintained areas. Kids will continue to play in these locations, but maybe they can be convinced not to play tag or other games that distract their attention from where they are.

Woods and Ravines

If your neighborhood has woods or a ravine, you should take a very close look. That means going right in, and walking around. You'll find that the places that would have made excellent forts when you were young are probably still active. Kids like to escape the adult world, and it's futile to try and stop them. However, it's nice to know where they're going. Is the tree fort safe? If not, the solution is not to tell your youngsters they can't use it. The best tactic is to explain why it isn't safe and to suggest ways to make it safe, or possibly to recommend tearing it down and making a new one. It's a privilege to visit a youngster's hideout. If you go in and destroy it, even for the best of reasons, you've probably cut off one area of communication. You simply won't hear about the next hideout. Your best bet is to go in with a genuine curiosity and interest. Tell your youngster about the secret places that you had when you were young. Compare yours with his. You'll have had tremendous success if you've located them and made them a safer place to be. You'll be glad to know where they are if you ever have to get hold of your youngster in an emergency.

A forest isn't the only place for a secret hideaway. Abandoned buildings are equally popular and often much more exciting and ultimately much more hazardous. A visit to one of these with your child should provide you with plenty of opportunities to demonstrate why it should be an off-limits location.

Traffic

However your kids get to their favorite places, there's no question that they'll have to cross streets, streets that are filled with preoccupied drivers. As a result, children should be taught not to count on drivers to obey the traffic signs. The lights may be red, or there may be a stop sign, but the child should be told not to step out until the vehicle has stopped.

As parents, we should realize that, just as we drift off, sometimes our kids do also. As a matter of fact, they probably spend as much time daydreaming as they do in the real world. If they're small, they may be pretending that the leaf on a puddle is actually a ship in a large ocean. At ten, they may be wondering whether or not they're going to make the school baseball team. Still later, they may be preoccupied with the boy or girl at the next desk. What's going on in their minds doesn't really matter. What's important is to recognize that mentally your child may not be where he or she is physically.

If you're not convinced, ask a child on the street a question. There's a reasonable chance that he or she will jump or will not hear you. Recognizing that they daydream is recognizing that this altered state makes them more vulnerable. You can help your child by talking about daydreaming and pointing out situations where the inherent dangers mean that the child should make a special attempt to pay attention. One way of doing this is to point out how exciting the street is. By pointing out areas of interest or how suddenly the street can change, you can help a youngster keep his or her mind on the street.

An opportunity to do this was provided by one of our snail-paced walks through the neighborhood. We were passing a street that we drove down regularly during the week. To our surprise, the street turned into a speed strip on the weekend. We had considered it one of the safer parts of our child's world. We pointed out to our youngster how wrong we had been to assume that we knew what was going on.

Shopping Malls and Plazas

Neighborhood shopping malls and plazas have in recent years become a significant part of many children's lives. There was no real equivalent when we were growing up. It's true that we hung out around the place where we bought sour grapes for a penny, but only in good weather. In the winter, when the store was standing-room only, we were chased home. Today, plazas provide warm, relatively unattended areas to hang out. Besides taking a close look at malls ourselves, we also talked to security people. Believe it or not, they report disturbances created by children as young as two or three. Older youngsters tend to fool around on the escalators, often running against the direction the stairs are moving. There have been serious injuries from kids falling head first. Teenagers are encouraged by the more hardened elements to try drugs. The problems are there all the time, but they are magnified after the stores close. Many malls stay open to accommodate the theater or restaurant crowd, and young people hanging around at these times are in danger of being picked up or molested. The more you talk with the security guards, the more convinced you become that, unless your youngsters are in a mall on a specific shopping trip, they shouldn't be there at all.

If you are with your child at a mall, you should inquire if there's a play center. These are supervised play areas where a youngster can stay while you're shopping. If your child is going to the mall on her own, she should be provided with a reasonable time limit.

Outside malls there are also problems. Parking lots and the large disposal bins found around malls and apartment buildings are dangerous play areas. No child is safe playing with refuse, and yet you often find them climbing around these huge bins. The parking lots in malls are safe in comparison to the ones in apartment buildings. Sometimes these extend two or more levels underground, and children should be taught to avoid them like the plague. Youngsters who live in high-rise apartments should also understand that the elevators are for transportation only. Kids playing in elevators can become a tremendous annoyance, and an unstable person might easily try to solve the problem with violence.

Terrain and Weather

Terrain forms an important part of your neighborhood. Paved hills are irresistible to skateboarders and roller skaters, and you can bet that if you haven't got an organized park, regular roadways will be used. If your child likes those sports, it might be worth setting up a car pool with his friends' parents. A regular trip to an organized location might eliminate the temptation to play chicken with automobiles. It's a game they can't win.

Of course, winter hills become great sliding locations. In

these situations, you must make sure that their path does not come close to trees, stumps, or a roadway.

A discussion of winter should remind you that weather can dramatically change your neighborhood. We were surprised when one of our youngsters returned home on a cold day in early April for his toy sailboat. Apparently, heavy rain and the spring runoff had combined to create a small lake behind the backed-up culvert. A visit to the impromptu regatta indicated a hazard that we'd never known about. We do now!

A person who's really concerned about streetproofing will pay special attention to water, frozen and not. It can be there one day and gone the next. When you're touring your neighborhood, be on the lookout for dry creeks. They'll deserve special attention in the spring.

Animals

A summary of a child's world would be incomplete without a knowledge of the local canine contingent. Though the breeds may vary, there's always the dog that loves every kid in the neighborhood. The animal believes it's human, goes everywhere with the gang, and licks everyone on the face. Don't ask where its tongue has been. There is also the scaredy-cat dog, usually small, that makes one hell of a racket and then runs away. Finally, there is the fierce dog, locked up in someone's backyard. No danger there, right? Wrong! In our neighborhood one of the friendliest dogs on the street was consistently teased by a group of children. One day it reached the end of its patience and, in its confusion, bit an innocent youngster. His stitches were out of his ankle in two weeks. By that time, man's best friend had been put to sleep. Some well-thought words of wisdom come far too late when you've got a youngster who's terrified of animals.

The best bet is to suggest that your children stay away from animals unless they are in the company of a friend who is the animal's owner. And even then, it's a better bet to leave them alone. Otherwise, even the most harmless situations can prove unpleasant. In a small town in Illinois, a rabid kitten wandered into a schoolyard. The kids adopted it and played with it for a few days. As a result of the adoption, 100 people had to undergo fourteen painful stomach injections.

Many youngsters feel the need to come to the aid of every animal in distress, from birds through skunks. Usually the parents are not aware of the situation until they're called to assist in minor or major surgery. By then the child is infected, and the animal is probably in worse trouble than it was before the rescue. As soon as your child is allowed to roam the neighborhood on his own, he should be instructed to call the Humane Society if he sees an animal in trouble. If for some reason he feels the animal must be moved, he should wear gloves before handling it.

People

Knowing your neighborhood animals is easy in comparison to knowing your neighborhood people. Teach your children to recognize the transient element—the strange person walking down the street, the bum in the park, or some punks hanging around a street corner—and to avoid them.

The next group you should concern yourself with is your youngster's peer group. Make an effort to meet your child's friends. It doesn't have to be an unpleasant task. As a matter of fact, it can be a great deal of fun. Do you know what your kid's friends like to do? Do you know the places where they meet with each other? Who's the guy or gal whose opinions mean the most to the rest of the group? You'll want to size that person up. If it's your own child, you're faced with some pretty specific questions. Only by knowing the neighborhood chums can you appreciate the kinds of pressures that your child is under. Only by understanding how they think can you have an insight into how your suggestions are being evaluated.

Finally, you should make every effort to know your neighborhood parents. Don't be afraid to introduce yourself. If your children are friends of the Smiths' youngsters, then they'll be over at the Smiths' home. There, they'll be following Smith rules, regulations and standards. What are Smith standards? Sometimes they're easy to figure out. The fourth time a young girl refuses her dinner after playing at a particular friend's house, it should become clear that those parents allow their children to eat between meals. That's a minor problem. You might learn, as we did, that a comparatively sedate family had some rather spicy video cassettes in their bedroom. Their eleven-year-old was adept with the Betamax, and while Mom cooked up preserves in the kitchen, her son was heating up their bedroom with a rather unemotional and somewhat confused family-life presentation. We learned about the blue movies when a particular youngster made a fuss because he'd been excluded from the afternoon session.

You shouldn't lie awake worrying about what goes on in your neighbors' bedrooms. However, you should talk with them about what your kids may and may not do.

Some kids are allowed to play in homes while their parents are out. If this is the case, you should know about it and make a decision as to your child's participation. Some families have power tools in the basement where the kids play. You can hope that these won't be touched, or you can do something about it. Some kids are allowed to drink wine with meals, and others are not. Sometimes the differences are as simple as parents having divergent opinions as to what they'll talk about in front of their kids. We heard about a particularly popular set of parents who were a lot less reserved in front of their children. That's fine if you approve, but it should be your choice. If your youngster is spending a lot of time with a particular friend, then you should make the effort to spend an evening with the parents. They may or may not turn out to be your favorite people, but that doesn't matter. If you can get to know each other, you'll be able to place what your children are telling you in perspective.

WHEN THE NEIGHBORHOOD CHANGES

Many parents are good about knowing their own neighborhood but make no effort to help their children if they find themselves in a new neighborhood, even for a short period of time. When two city children drown in a farm pond belonging to relatives, everybody feels sick at heart. And yet how many of us set down the ground rules for our youngsters when we are at a new location? The farm was a strange neighborhood for the two youngsters who died. They didn't realize that the mud banks of a pond can be soft and can give way. One youngster slid into the water and the other drowned in an attempt to save the first one. Because the neighborhood looked harmless to the adults, there was probably little attempt to wander around it with the kids before leaving them to go off on their own.

Parents can't know the hazards in every location, but if they don't, they should either tour the area themselves or get together with the children and someone familiar with the new neighborhood. Where youngsters are in a totally new environment, they shouldn't be allowed to go off exploring alone.

The same rule must apply to country kids who are in the city for the first time. Whether they're truly from the country or have lived their lives in a small town or a quiet suburb, they should take special care during their first few city experiences. The number of people and the speed of the activity can cause a youngster to panic. The transit system they're traveling on for the first time may be supervised, but that will not be of help to a child who isn't sure where he came from, let alone where he's going.

To streetproof your child, you need to assume that your child knows nothing about the street. You must also recognize that it has changed a lot since you were there. Moreover, since the neighborhood will grow as your child grows, you must remain vigilant and be aware of changes. Just as your child makes new friends and discards old ones, your neighborhood will lose some people and gain others.

An area can also change with the seasons. Depending on where you live, certain seasons may bring more hazards than others. By walking with your child, you can eliminate the mystery inherent in a forbidden location or find dangers in seemingly benign ones. If you aren't part of your child's world, it's tough to set guidelines. You'll find your child will be more likely to follow them if you've taken the time to demonstrate to him the reasons behind the rules. Walk your neighborhood, see it, know it. When you do, your streetproofing program will have begun.

3

EARLY-WARNING SYSTEMS FOR YOU AND YOUR CHILD

You can't watch your children every minute of every day, and the time you can physically see them becomes shorter as they move from house to sidewalk to street to playground and into the neighborhood. As they grow, so will their boundaries and so must mutual trust. In fact, without mutual trust you would not be streetproofing your children; you would be crippling them.

By establishing a basis of trust ahead of time, you can ensure that something of you and your love goes with your child even when he's away from you. By learning to read what's not being said, and what is being said through behavior and actions, you can create an early-warning system that can alert you to dangers before they get out of hand.

Creating an early-warning system for your children and yourselves is a family project. No matter how large or small your family, the system will work best if members of all ages participate. All you need is a little time and heightened powers of observation.

Use the time to teach your children to see what's going on around them. That's the first step. Once they can see, you can teach them to react to situations in a positive and constructive way. But you're not off the hook—you must also learn to pay close attention to what's being said to you. Let's face it; it's a two-way street and everyone has to cooperate.

LEARN TO COMMUNICATE

The only real way you'll ever know what's going on in your child's world is by having him tell you. But all too often we ask the same repetitive questions and never take the time to really listen or explore what's being said, or, more importantly, not said. It's almost like asking a passing acquaintance how he is; you don't really wait for an answer. You expect to hear, "Fine, thanks."

The main reason parents don't know their children is because they tend to view their children's lives as boring. They are not really interested. But we believe that you'd better get interested.

The fact is, many of the things your children do are things you've done a thousand times before. There's no question that the events themselves have lost some of their interest. However, it's *your* youngster who's doing something for the first time. The trick is to focus less on the event and more on your child's thoughts and emotions.

Parents who concentrate on how many goals their youngster scored are focusing on the event. Parents who ask their children if they enjoyed the competition, or if they were scared when they first stepped on the ice, are concentrating on the child. If you can follow this second example, then your child will feel more valued. He will also learn to trust you with his real feelings on a subject. You may be surprised to learn that your child's reactions to various events are quite different from the ones you had when you were young. In addition, they might put the event in a whole new perspective for you.

The best way to improve your communications with your child is to try to remember those areas where you had poor communication with your parents. If you can think back and analyze why you had trouble talking about these things, you may find some clues that will help you to communicate better. By improving your communications, we feel that you can know your child better and therefore do a better job of streetproofing.

Lies

When you're talking with your children you've got to remember that in some situations they are going to be tempted to tell you what they think you want to hear. Some people might say that kids will lie. We believe that kids will generally color the truth in order to make their behavior more reasonable. If you can recognize the situations in which this might occur, you can counteract it so that your child doesn't come to believe that dishonesty is an effective means of existence.

Recognizing the situations where youngsters might change the truth is simply a question of stretching your mind back to your own childhood. If you were shy, you might remember the temptation to say that you understood something when you did not. Is that a lie? Well, whether it is or not, it's perfectly understandable. However, it can lead to problems and possibly real lies. The best way to eliminate this problem is to take the time to ask your child to repeat your explanation or instructions. If she stumbles, then you should carefully explain again. Whatever you do, don't get annoyed at a youngster who's slow to understand something. If you've failed to communicate, then the responsibility and the blame are yours.

Kids don't always think of consequences of their actions. Parents who insist that their children provide explanations for everything they do may be overlooking this simple fact, and forcing their children to make up a story just for the sake of form. If children become used to this, they'll get into the habit of having long and complicated explanations, and it will become increasingly hard for them to tell the truth.

It's not only the request for explanations that can cause children to color the truth. If they anticipate that they're always going to get a no by telling the truth, they may provide you with what you want to hear in order to get a yes. Parents should try and avoid the automatic no. While there are some requests where no is the only alternative, a child is more likely to accept them if he feels that there was at least an equal chance of a yes in the situation.

Most parents accept what are referred to as white lies. These are explained as situations where a slight fib has been told in order not to hurt someone. As far as we're concerned, kids should be taught to tell the truth on all occasions, and they definitely shouldn't be punished for doing so. If they learn to trust you when they are telling you the truth, then your communications, and your understanding of each other, should improve dramatically.

However, if you catch a child telling a lie, try to understand the purpose of the lie, and explain your reason for being upset. There are plenty of good "street" reasons you can give. If, for example, your youngster told you that he was going bowling with a friend and instead went to a restricted movie, explain that you wouldn't have been able to get in touch with him in case of an emergency at home. Or, if he got in trouble, you wouldn't have been able to help if you didn't know where he'd last been. Encourage your kids to admit they were wrong if they do something stupid. Don't put them in the position of having to create a phony explanation if there isn't one.

As a parent, you can set an example. Don't feel that you have to be perfect in front of your child. If you do something that's wrong, admit it. If there was no reason for the stupidity, don't make one up. If you expect the truth, you'd better be prepared to give it.

An Honest Relationship

If you're both honest and open with each other, you'll have gone a long way toward streetproofing your youngster, and you'll find her a much more interesting person to spend time with. You'll have a much warmer and more honest relationship if you stop treating your children as acquaintances and start treating them as good friends, whose conversation you find interesting and informative. Plan time to discuss the day's events with your children. Share events from your day; don't just wait to tell your husband or wife. Engage your children in your life and they will open up about theirs. Ask them questions that require broader information and you will find yourself in a position to share the events and people involved in their day. You can find out with whom they were playing, where they were playing, and what they were playing.

If you found out your child was playing doctor with Bill and Judy in Bill's basement, it would tell you a lot. First, that there's some question as to how much supervision there is at Bill's house. Second, that someone's natural curiosity about the body is starting to awaken. Here, gentle questioning can determine whose.

The third thing you can learn is that your child is more than willing to talk to you if the right questions are asked in the right way. It would be a good idea to ask how the game of doctor is played, to give you more information as to what's going on. You might also wish to know who initiated the game. This should be done in a conversational manner, remembering that even if you don't like what you hear, your child felt comfortable enough to tell you—so don't overreact. After all, the game could have changed over the years.

The simple point here is that the more you encourage your children to talk to you, the more knowledge you will have about their activities away from the home. This will pay off later as their social horizons widen.

OLDER CHILDREN

If you're dealing with older youngsters, the same process is valid, with one exception—their privacy may become an even greater factor. With this in mind, pick a time for conversation that will provide a one-on-one situation. This does not mean that the open form of question should be stopped: open conversation should always be encouraged. It does mean that you should be sensitive to your child's need for privacy. In your one-on-one conversation you should make it perfectly clear that yes, it is private; and yes, you will respect your child's trust; but he or she must understand that you will make the final decision as to when to share the confidentiality. On these occasions, however, you should explain why you're sharing it.

Here's an exercise that we found helped get the conversation going. Take the old question "What did you do in school today?" Now think of five different ways of engaging your child in conversation that will elicit the same information but without asking a dead-end question. For example, if you start your conversation on a positive note, such as, "You look as though you had a pretty good day today," you let your child know you have a conversation, not an inquisition, in mind. Remember that if your children have been on what they perceive as a reporting basis with you, they may at first be reluctant to take you up on your offer of two-way communication. Don't get discouraged; if one avenue is closed, try another. Ask their opinion on some matter; involve them in the decision-making processes, especially when it concerns some aspect of their personal world. Everything that affects us ultimately affects them, so include them whenever you can.

Children love solving problems; they especially love to feel they have contributed to the family in a positive way. Once they have the feeling that their opinions are valued, the question "What did you do in school today?" ceases to be a dead-end question and becomes an invitation to talk. Talking involves information sharing, idea sharing, and, most of all, time sharing. The time is well worth spending. Remember they're your kids and the best thing you can invest in them is your time. You can't streetproof children if you don't know what's going on in their heads, and there's nothing like conversation to help you find out.

WHAT TO TALK ABOUT

Once you're all chattering like a bunch of magpies, here are some things you're going to want to encourage them to talk to you about.

What do they think is strange behavior in others?

We walked through several neighborhoods, just watching the behavior of adults. On some days we were sure the nuts had taken over: we saw people talking to themselves, people going through strange actions, and people just standing, staring at something we couldn't see. Yes, the world was nuts and we were never letting our children out of the house again.

But then we started to think; we wanted to streetproof our children, not lock them up. What we had seen was strange behavior, yes, but was it threatening behavior? Was it dangerous to our children? We quickly realized that if we couldn't answer that question, we could turn them into paranoid little children who jumped at the sight of their own shadows. And to answer it, we did a lot of walking and a lot of talking.

This is what it comes down to—find out what your children think about the behavior of others. If they find it strange that someone talks to himself, encourage them to tell you about it. It will give you a golden opportunity to explain that there is a difference between someone who talks to himself and a stranger who follows them but never says a word. Remember, the more you listen, the more you can teach them; and the more you encourage, the more you can learn.

How do they feel about the behavior of people—kids and adults—whom they know?

By understanding why they like or dislike someone, you can get a picture of the social makeup of your child's world. But remember that it changes hourly, so a once-a-week checkup isn't good enough. It's an ongoing process.

You should also pay attention to the things that are not said. As you learn to listen more attentively, you'll notice that people and places that were of high interest last week have faded completely from today's conversation, having been replaced by new people and new places. This is normal—we all have passing interests—but with children it can tell you when they've changed friends and areas of play. As we explained in "Know Your Neighborhood," if it is a person or place you don't know, check it out.

Learning Whom to Trust

Of course, it's one thing to get your children to share their feelings about their peers and another to encourage them to express emotions or observations about adults—especially authority figures and people they love. But you have to encourage them to tell you about any concerns they have about the actions of anyone, including teachers, family members and your friends. The single most important thing to remember is that if you ever overreact to what they have told you, you could slam the door of trust that you've worked so hard to open.

It's a terrible thing to realize that someone you trust could tamper with your child. But it has happened to one of our children, and that experience brought home to us an understanding that the child must be held guiltless. Your anger is not what they need: they need love and comfort. If your child has the courage and trust it takes to tell you, then you've created a bond that is ongoing for life.

We found the best way of dealing with this problem is to explain, in their language, where people can touch them and where they cannot. In other words, set body boundaries. And anyone who breaks the boundaries is then questioned about it by you. It's as simple as that.

In most cases, children seem to think that certain people—teachers, close family friends and relatives—can take liberties with them, because they have some authority or special rights. After all, kids have been trained to obey adults. But in your conversations you have the opportunity to teach them that there are times when it's all right to go against an adult's wishes. They should be taught that if it does not seem right, they should follow their own feelings and come to you. Encourage them to tell you and then reassure them that you support them.

In developing your early-warning system, you will want your child to develop a strong belief that if it doesn't seem right to her, it's all right to question it.

What is acting nice?

By asking a question that will allow your child to think positively, you encourage him to participate. Then you have the opportunity to move to the subject you want to discuss.

What is acting not nice?

Just follow this line as an example.

> "What is not nice?"
> "When Johnny throws stones."
>
> "Right. What else?"
> "When Sara picks her nose."
>
> "Well, yes, that's not too nice. It's better to blow it, right?"
> "Yes."
>
> "What about if a man wants to give you candy. Is that nice?"
> "Yes."
>
> "Why?"
> "Because he likes me."

"But what if you don't know him?"

"Well, he's just nice. He wants to share."

"Well, he might want to share, but don't you think he should ask me if it's all right to share his candy? He could come right here and say, 'I would like to share my candy with Robin because she's very nice.'"

"He might not know where I live."

"Well, if he doesn't know where you live, he doesn't know you and he's not really very nice if he gets you in trouble for taking candy from someone we don't know."

"But he might know where I live."

"Yes, he might—but would he be acting nice if he told a lie?"

"No."

"That's right, he wouldn't be acting nice. And he might be lying to you just to get you away from your friends."

Learning What To Do in Emergencies

If you encourage your child to counter your argument with all her questions in this way, you can often tell how she's reasoning. You then know how to deal with the clues as to how she would react in certain situations. With this information in hand, you can deal with her style of logic in terms she will understand.

Of course, there is another benefit from this kind of dialogue: it gives the child practice in verbalizing her feelings and sharing information. It helps her become more capable and confident in dealing with situations that could arise, should she ever be lost or required to impart information to the authorities.

Time spent communicating with your children can instill in them a confidence that will allow them to trust their own feelings. But it doesn't stop there. You also have to be willing to give them information about yourself and how you would behave in certain situations.

Take, for instance, an emergency. How would you let them know they were supposed to go with someone? You've already explained why they should not go with someone they don't know, and you've encouraged them to always check with you first, even if they do know the person. But do they know what *you* would do in an emergency? Tell them how you would get in touch with them if the need arose. Let them know by whom and how they would be contacted. Discuss the alternatives and finally give them names and numbers of people with whom they could check if they were still in doubt. If they are in school or at a friend's house, it's relatively easy for them to check. If they're at the playground, they should have some way of knowing that you have, in fact, approved their going with the person in question—no matter who it is.

Your goal is obviously not to make them suspicious and untrusting, but rather self-sufficient and streetwise. You can actually increase their sense of security by giving them guidelines on when to be suspicious and when not to be. The world is a big place, and there are dangers in it that may not be obvious to them. The more they know, the wiser they'll be.

Playing "What If"

Another way to reinforce the system is by role playing. Make it a family exercise and play "what if." Children learn through play, and they like nothing better than playing with you. Test their understanding by setting up situations and then playing them out. For example, say "What if I wanted you home from the park?" Then act out the situation.

First send a stranger. They should know that you would never send a stranger to get them at the park.

Next send Uncle Fred. Now don't throw your hands up in horror; it happens and you know it, and your children should know that if Uncle Fred doesn't know the password or have a card they would recognize, they should go to the nearest safe place and call you—or they should know that it is planned that Uncle Fred will pick them up.

Play out situations; have fun. They'll enjoy it and you'll reinforce the system in their minds.

There is one more consideration that is important to your family's early-warning system. That is the neighborhood at large. We suggest that you let your neighbors know how the general system works. Not, of course, your own family's code or passwords—that information must be kept private. But open up lines of communication between other parents and yourselves. Become involved in what's going on in your community. It's very reassuring for your children to see you out walking or talking to other people in their world. It will create a strong sense of belonging and a trust that you are there.

BE OBSERVANT

Having opened a clear channel of communications and laid down procedures of contact, we come to your powers of observation. You don't have to spy; simply be observant and watch just what's going on in your child's world. Notice what comes into your house and what goes out—what's new and what's old.

Let's first deal with the younger child. Take, for instance, the day your six-year-old comes in to get the hammer. Why? Where is he going with it? What is he going to do with it? Well, obviously he is going to hammer, but on what and with what? Nails? Take a minute to find out where he's going and with whom. Is it a place you've checked out, a place you approve of, a place such as the fort? If the children have a hammer, what other tools do they have that could be potentially more dangerous? By watching what your children are playing with, you will have a pretty good idea as to where and what they're playing.

Toy Boxes

We also strongly suggest you make it your business to know the contents of their toy boxes. All too often we think we know, but, in reality, toy boxes can contain objects never before seen by us, objects that could be potentially dangerous.

A great exercise is to have regular room and playroom cleanouts. By helping your child on the cleanout day, you can get a pretty good idea of just what she has accumulated unbeknownst to you. At the same time, you won't be invading her privacy by snooping while she's out.

Money

As your children get older and allowance or odd-job incomes become part of their world, you should always be aware of just how much money they really do have, including birthday, Christmas or special-occasion gifts. You should also know just what things cost in the marketplace— how much albums cost, how much the latest toy being promoted on television costs. If, for the sake of discussion, your son has five dollars spending money a week and he's arriving home with a new album every Saturday, that has got to tell you something. It will if you know that the price of an album these days far exceeds five dollars.

Children do trade and they do occasionally buy things on sale or at bargain prices, but if you are aware of going prices and just how much money your children have to spend, you can easily spot trouble before it gets a head start.

Should you find some objects coming into the house that

would suggest your child has spent more money than you believe he possesses, stay calm. Don't offend his dignity by making an accusation of wrongdoing before you've investigated and confirmed your suspicions. Even then you should approach him with understanding and, above all, an open mind. Give him a chance to explain his side of the case. In the end, firm action may be called for, depending, of course, on the source of the extra money or items themselves.

It doesn't matter how the money or items were obtained. It makes no difference if it was by stealing, borrowing or dealing in drugs. The first time is the only time to stop it, and your actions in the first instance will be the ones he will remember. Be fair but firm, and follow through whatever course of action is appropriate. It may involve the police, restitution, or paying back borrowed money. The main thing is while you stand beside him, make him responsible for his actions. He will thank you in the end.

One last word on this: should something of this nature occur in your family, don't ostracize the offender. Show him you still love him and respect him. Don't shut down communications; keep talking; keep being a family. An early-warning system is no good if it only works once, then halts operations. An early-warning system is built on mutual trust, personal visibility, open communications, and some clearly defined procedures. It takes time and energy to keep it operating.

4
PEOPLEPROOFING YOUR CHILD

As soon as your children are on the street and away from your supervision, they will be faced with the necessity of sizing up people on their own. Peopleproofing your children for the street means providing them with some ground rules for making judgments about the behavior of others. Can I trust this person? Is she being honest with me? Why is he behaving that way?

No matter how sophisticated a child appears, it's probably best to assume that he is pretty gullible. His basic criterion for judging other people is whether or not those other people are nice to him. This isn't a bad starting point but, as every adult knows, it's not a good finishing point.

We've all made people mistakes. Sometimes we've trusted those we shouldn't have, and other times we've been embarrassed to learn that someone we've been wary of was filled with the purest of motives. Because of our errors, we often shy away from all but the most superficial generalizations.

"Johnny, I don't want to see you talking with that man again."

"What man, Mother?"

"The one who sits in the park and drinks cheap sherry."

No parent would disagree with Johnny's mother on this point, but beyond that, where do you go in order to provide your children with useful advice?

When we were talking with the police, they told us a story that crystallized the problem. It seems that a young girl had been abducted. In an attempt to get background information on the story, a newspaper reporter had gone to a number of schoolyards to talk to the children. Of the twenty-five six- and seven-year-olds he spoke to, only one refused to talk. All the others carefully explained that their parents had instructed them never to speak to strangers. Having done this, they proceeded with the interviews. Apparently, a man in a shirt and tie who says he is a reporter does not qualify as a stranger. Strangers for youngsters look similar to the bum drinking sherry. If you watch the papers, you may conclude that he's far more harmless than the respectable gentleman in the suit.

RECOGNIZING STRANGERS

So, what's a stranger? A young child will tell you that it's a person he's never met. "So when you meet somebody for the first time they're a stranger, right?"

"That's right."

If you pursue this line of questioning, you'll discover that your child probably doesn't consider a person a stranger after two or three more meetings. If the person seems nice after this many encounters, then he is to be trusted . . . or is he?

You have to tread a fine line here. While you clearly don't want your children to be suspicious of everybody, you do want them to develop a healthy skepticism. Developing it will be a process as unique to your family as your philosophical beliefs. However, we can give you some ground rules and guidelines; by discussing them, we hope you will define your own.

Some parents say, "Make sure the people you meet earn your respect and friendship." This is done, they say, by "showing you respect and friendship." The message is sort of a reversed golden rule. The next step is to give examples. Capitalize on the opportunities in which you can say, "The reason we don't trust so and so is because . . ." It's important, when attempting this, to explain your method of judging. While example is a good teacher, circumstance may cloud the message for your kids. If, on the other hand, they understand your reasoning, they will be able to apply it more quickly when they are on the street.

All adults have cues and signals they use to evaluate others. Discuss yours. Provide your children with some guidelines on how to judge the people they meet. First, try to provide them with a basic understanding of what is normal or natural behavior. For example, many people are somewhat ill at ease in their initial contacts with new people. Tell your kids that this is normal. For someone to appear shy, or possibly a little silly or flippant, is not unusual.

Beware of Flatterers

Next, explain what they should be wary of. We've all heard the old expression "Flattery will get you nowhere." Though as an adult, I've changed it to "Flattery may get you everywhere," you should tell your child that if he meets someone who spends too much time telling him what a great person he is, he should be on his guard. Though this may not happen to youngsters often, they're certainly subjected to the reverse. Those are people who spend a great deal of time telling a young person how wonderful they personally are. Children should ask themselves why a person is doing this. It's our opinion that if a person is coming on too strong, then a child can conclude they're trying to sell something. The challenge, then, is to identify what it is.

Information, Please

Another type whom we've all met at one time or another is the individual who wishes to know everything about you while providing virtually no background on himself. Kids should be taught that it's inadvisable to tell their life story to total strangers. If, in the long run, the person earns their friendship, there'll be plenty of time for swapping family histories. A person who refuses to give a little for what she gets may well be hiding a past that she is not proud of. It's important to explain to a youngster that someone who is ashamed of her past should have her offer of friendship considered very carefully.

Remind your child that friendships, good friendships, take a long time to create: they don't happen overnight. We must be careful not to send our children mixed messages on this matter. We must examine our own use of the word *friend.* We sometimes refer to people we've only met twice as "my friend." We feel you should teach your child the difference between the words *acquaintance* and *friend,* that the people you just meet once or twice are merely acquaintances, while the people you enjoy being with and see regularly are your friends.

Children hear and see much more of what parents say and do than we sometimes realize, and they model their actions on the total image, not just the parts we want them to. So we must all be careful not to seem like the people we're trying to teach them to be cautious of. We were told a story by a friend that points up the problem graphically. Our friend's wife was trying to teach their boy that the policeman was his friend, that he was a friend to the whole family and could be trusted. The only comment the little boy had was "Well, how come he never comes to the house for drinks or dinner?" That started a whole new tack of peopleproofing by explaining the difference between acquaintances, helping friends, and personal friends, a difference we all too often ignore by dumping too many people into the friend category without any explanation or thought as to how it will affect our children.

Pressure Tactics

The next type of individual your child should be wary of doesn't tell your youngster he's wonderful, doesn't go on about himself, and doesn't hide his background. As a matter of fact, he is quite forthright during the initial contact. However, he may want your child to do something that is against his will. It could be a borderline proposition, like going for a nature hike in a ravine. It might even be legitimate. Where the interaction goes off the tracks is when your child feels pressured to make an immediate decision in case he misses "this great opportunity." Kids should understand that good people will respect them even if they're confused about what they should do in a particular situation. Explain that it's normal for people to be provided with an appropriate amount of time to make up their minds. Tell your youngster that if he is having difficulty evaluating the alternatives, you want him to discuss them with you. Kids need to understand that a nice person making a reasonable request will not mind in the slightest if parents are consulted.

Equal Input

The next lesson a youngster should learn is the equal input theorem. Kids should be taught to ask themselves what the relationship means for the other person. The best way to bring the idea out is to ask them if they'd be really interested in playing with someone who is substantially younger than they are. If they look at you as though they think you've lost your mind, then discuss the reverse possibility with them. What would they think if someone substantially older wanted to spend a great deal of time in their company? The general point is that children of similar ages usually have similar interests. If an adult is still fascinated by what kids are up to, there may be something wrong. You can point out that there are, of course, exceptions. An older person may love telling stories to young kids. In this situation the kids learn about someone's life, and the older person has the pleasure of being valued and needed. But if an older person wants to play with your child, and your youngster can't figure out why, then he should discuss it with you.

These, and other rules you will think up, should help a youngster avoid problems. While they may occasionally cut the child off from normal interaction, we believe that, at best, they'll cause the child to slow down and think, and that's not bad.

DANGEROUS SITUATIONS

When should kids be particularly careful? Well, when they're vulnerable. A child is more vulnerable than you are, and must therefore take added precautions. Though all children have a sense of their own vulnerablity—that is, why they're frightened in certain situations—they rarely use it as a means of evaluating how they should behave. As a result, it's something that adults should discuss with them.

Cars

If your seven-year-old is walking along the street and a car stops to ask her for directions, she should understand that she is vulnerable. Therefore, she should be alert and stay well out of reach of the person. If she knows the direction, she's welcome to provide a polite answer. However, if the driver asks to be taken to the location, she should refuse the request. If you walk children through this scenario, it makes more sense to them than a statement such as "Don't talk to strangers." As a result, they're more likely to take you seriously.

If, on the other hand, a woman stranger asks a group of four fifteen-year-olds to help her change a tire, we'd all agree they should. As you find yourself around the streets with your children, play the game of "would you do this?" By creating various situations, you can help them appreciate when they are more and less vulnerable and, as a result, when they should be more on their guard.

New Friends

This vulnerability, however, is not limited to cars and tires. It exists for kids when they encounter a person they know in a new environment. If your youngster has only met a child in class, he should be wary when he first goes home with that friend. When I was young, I knew another young boy at school. When I first went to his house, I was shocked to find that he owned a bullwhip, which he proceeded to flick dangerously close to my face. I was genuinely frightened, and though the event did not result in injury, I avoided being alone with the boy from then on.

A friend of ours related a similar experience. As a teenager, he visited a very popular teacher at his home. In retrospect, he knew he was fortunate not to have been confronted with a rather unfortunate sexual advance. Again, the facts are simple: people are not always the same in one environment as they are in another.

Traveling

The second place where young people are particularly vulnerable is when they are traveling. As we mention in Chapter 7, young people love to travel. Traveling is one of the most important experiences of growing up. However, your children should be made aware of the fact that travel creates artificial circumstances, such as a strong friendship because two people both perceive themselves as vulnerable in a strange place. Travel is exciting for young people because they feel that in getting away from home they are also escaping the rules and regulations their parents impose. A youngster on his own in a new city feels all the exhilaration of being an adult for the very first time and suffers none of the uncertainty. Moreover, those adults who are likely to take advantage of young people can spot the new travelers as clearly as you can spot a five-year-old telling a fib. This makes the young traveler particularly vulnerable.

Traveling can also be lonely, and lonely young people will make friends very easily. If someone needs a friend badly, he is not always as choosy as he might be at home. Again, this increases the vulnerability inherent in the situation.

The third fact that should be mentioned to kids who are going to travel abroad is that the rules away from home may not be the same as they are at home. As a result, kids should be encouraged to behave cautiously in new circumstances until they've had a chance to see how people act.

Acknowledging the problems is not suggesting that young people should avoid travel. However, if you have a budding Marco Polo in your own family, you should definitely discuss the potential hazards. Travel is an adventure that demands continuous alertness. As it's tough to be bright all the time, we suggest that travel is preferable if done in a group. Certainly, two people paying attention is better than one.

Cult Tactics

Another area you should discuss with your children is cult tactics. They may have no trouble dealing with an individual who simply stuffs a pamphlet into their hands as they walk along the street. But some cults use tactics that are much more devious. They are often experts at engaging people, especially young people, in conversation. While some cult members wear robes or shave their heads, many aren't readily recognizable. In fact, in most instances, they don't at first even mention religion or beliefs at all. They just come on like nice people offering a little friendship to another person. Your youngster should be aware of how they operate and what they're really after.

If your child is approached on the street, or anywhere else

for that matter, he should be warned to look for the signs that will clue him into the situation. He should know how the approach works and that it is never, or at least very seldom, a direct offering of friendship. It comes in many disguises, but one of the most popular is the request for directions to a certain house or storefront not far from where contact is first made. It then moves to the fact that it's a place where the supposedly lost individual is meeting some friends and that it's a great place to grab a coffee, listen to a little music, and rap—and best of all, it's free.

But before the recruiter will ask your child if he would like to join him, he will introduce himself and generally be pretty open. He'll engage in conversation until he thinks the moment is right and then make the invitation. Another twist he might throw in is the observation that "you look pretty down, and I know you don't know me, but if you want to grab a coffee I'm a good listener." Sound transparent and obvious? Well, it is. But brought into play at the right time on the right kid, it can work. Remember, if a child feels alone and rejected or ignored at home, and someone is willing to share his troubles, anything is better than nothing. After all, no one is asking him to go to some out-of-the-way place; they're just offering a coffee or coke and some conversation. What harm can that do?

Don't believe for a minute that the cults just look for the misfits. Their philosophy is based on the theory that if you throw a large enough net, you're bound to catch at least one fish. They operate wherever kids gather, and they may take weeks before they actually approach someone. Even then it's a slow, warm, nonthreatening kind of approach. Tactics vary, even within a cult. Sometimes they'll use a two-on-one approach; other times they'll offer something free. But what they like the best are curious kids who feel that they can handle anything the recruiter can throw at them. We recommend you inform your children about cults and how they may try to make contact. They should understand that people who come on to them while waiting for a friend on the corner are up to something and quite pointedly want something. If they take a pamphlet to read while waiting, just for something to do, warn them that the person who comes up to ask them how they like it is probably on the make for their mind.

We teach our children from their earliest days not to talk to strangers. But when your youngsters reach their midteens, they're very nearly adults and you can expect them to start making some independent decisions as to whom they'll talk to and when. What you can do before they reach that stage is to educate them about people.

GETTING HELP

Despite all your efforts to keep your children out of harm's way, they could still find themselves in a dangerous situation involving an attack on their person. This brings us to an interesting topic in terms of peopleproofing. When does a youngster run, and when does he fight? It's our opinion that in every possible circumstance, he should try to get away if he finds himself in an awkward situation. Later on, we'll deal with where he should look for help. However, we believe strongly that discretion is the better part of valor.

Assuming that circumstances make it impossible for your child to get away, he should try to make as much noise as possible. Whether he does this by screaming or kicking over a garbage can doesn't matter. He should be taught to draw as much attention as possible. There are now air-pressure and electronic noisemakers on the market that anyone can carry. You may want to provide your children with them. The important thing to stress is that they must not panic. No matter how nervous they may feel inside, they must teach themselves to stay calm and to rationally decide what course of action to follow.

Police

Clearly, the first place that a young person should look for help is with the police. An unfortunate development in our society has been the loss of respect for the police. Recently, we read in a newspaper a letter from a policeman: "When I'm in a restaurant or store with parents whose small children are misbehaving and causing a fuss, the parents will say, 'If you don't behave yourself I'm going to call that cop over here, and he will take you away and lock you up!' The parents may not realize it, but they are putting the fear of the police into the children's heads and making the law officer out to be a bad man—a person to be hated and feared. It's hard enough for us to gain the respect of children today without having this kind of image to fight. A child who is lost needs to know that the police officer is his friend, and is there to help."

The letter speaks for itself. However, you can help children gain respect by taking some positive actions. If you're walking with your child, and you pass a policeman on the beat, talk to him. That will demonstrate to your child that you respect him. You can also explain to your children that the policeman is probably a parent just like you. If young children can realize that police are parents too, it will make the officers much more approachable.

Police, of course, may not always be available exactly when they are needed. As a result, you should discuss a list of best bets for a crisis situation.

Others In Uniform

The first line of help after the police is other uniformed people. Soldiers would be a possibility in this case, but it's more likely that your child could contact a crossing guard or a postman. If your child is on a public transit vehicle, or in a public transit station, he'd be smart to get the attention of a driver or other transit employee. Most transit vehicles are equipped with bells, or emergency alarms, and you should point these out to your youngsters. It's better to have them turn in a false alarm and risk a fine than to get into real trouble. This also holds true for any other alarm they may encounter in times of difficulty.

Even if people are busy doing their job, your children should be instructed to interrupt them if they believe they are in trouble. Better to take the chance of creating a minor annoyance than to discover that the situation has become unmanageable as a result of their failure to ask someone for help.

CBers

Another good bet is provided by people with radios. A cab driver can radio for help if a child is in trouble, and of course he can also drive the youngster home in case of a real emergency. As well, children can be taught to seek help from people who have CB radios mounted on their vehicles. However, they should first check that the vehicle has call letters or a club decal prominently mounted. These generally indicate that the driver is responsible, and it makes it easy to identify the vehicle at a later date.

Children should be told in emergency situations to memorize and write down the license numbers, call numbers or any other distinguishing marks of vehicles involved in the situation. In many cases, license numbers have led to the apprehension of criminals.

Naturally, you must create your own list of people your children should trust. However, here are some others you might wish to consider. They can look for anybody who is performing a job activity. Included in this list would be shopkeepers, and gas station attendants. Of course, other people with children are generally a safe bet.

THE LAST RESORT

If it's dark and your child finds himself in a crisis situation, he should be told to run anywhere where there are lights or people. Unfortunately, a situation may arise in which your children are physically threatened and cannot simply run away. The point is you should also discuss with your children what their alternatives are, if they are grabbed and the attacker is not after their possessions. While it is an unpleasant topic, it's one that you should not ignore. The fact is that if your child is grabbed, he or she has probably broken one of the streetproofing rules.

After emphasizing that anything you discuss is only to be used as a last resort, you could begin the conversation by asking what they might do if someone grabbed them. A younger child may well have few alternatives but to go along. However, they are not the only ones who are vulnerable. Your fifteen-year-old boy may believe that he is pretty tough. The fact is that if he genuinely encounters someone who is in the criminal element, he may find out that this person does not play by Marquis of Queensbury rules. For anyone in this situation, the first choice should be to take some action that might allow him to get away.

One of the best ways is to spin in much the same way that a good football halfback does. A person who really spins hard is very hard to hold on to. To see how it works, you might grab your child and let him practice different ways of trying to spin out of your arms.

Another technique that can work extremely well is to dive to the ground and roll. A person who is rolling on the ground is very hard to grab, and believe it or not, it's also difficult for anyone to punch or kick someone who is rolling quickly. Again, to have a sense of how this might work, you might try it out with your son or daughter. The test should be done out of doors.

A simple trick that you can practice with your children is

having them go completely limp. As anyone knows from trying to carry a sleeping child of any size, dead weight is extremely hard to cope with.

In all these examples the basic message for all youngsters is to keep their body as low as possible, for this makes it extremely difficult for anyone to manhandle them. The person would have to bend over to pick the child up and, as a consequence, would be off balance, making it possible to push him over.

Children can be taught to fight only as a very last resort, if they feel their life is threatened. It's an individual judgment that parents must make for themselves. However, with the number of ultimately tragic abductions that you see in the paper, most parents would opt for a bruised or scratched child over one who was permanently lost. If youngsters are going to fight, they should use absolutely anything at their disposal. As the chances of their landing a good blow are extremely slim, they should resort to whatever is available.

In Toronto, Ontario, a gritty teen foiled a holdup man. Though she was only five feet four inches tall, the seventeen-year-old bit a would-be robber, knocked him off balance, and sent him running from a hardware store during an afternoon holdup attempt. She said that the robber grabbed her, but before he could demand money, she started screaming. He responded by shoving two fingers in her mouth, and she did what comes naturally—she chomped down on them as hard as she could. The bandit threw her to the floor, and when he came toward her with a gun, she knocked him off balance. "The last I saw of him, he was running in the other direction."

One very smart fourteen-year-old girl had another answer. She stuck her finger down her throat and threw up on her attacker. He was so put off, he fled.

Not every youngster will be that brave, or that lucky. As a parent, you've got to evaluate your children's temperaments and provide them with advice that you think they're capable of following. However, just because you believe that your child is timid, you shouldn't ignore situations such as the attempted hardware store holdup. Everybody reacts differently under pressure, and just hearing how something worked might save a child's life.

Peopleproofing your child cannot be done overnight. As a parent, you must pick your times to cover various areas, but make sure you cover them all. Talking about why your children like and dislike certain other children might be an opportunity for discussing how you evaluate people. On the other hand, a play fight might provide the perfect opportunity for discussing various evasive techniques.

However you choose to peopleproof your kids, make sure that you emphasize that the majority of people are good souls just like you.* While there is definitely a danger of not perceiving threats that are very real, there is a chance that children will not trust people when they should. Though one tends to remember the dramatic events from one's youth, there's no question that there are literally hundreds of times as many good people as bad, and it's important to recognize them. That's not so difficult if your kids are with people from a similar background. Where it's tricky is when they meet someone from a substantially different background. Everybody feels slightly threatened by people who have a different view of the world from theirs. However, there are a lot of different ways of doing the right thing in this world, and one of your jobs as a parent is to explain that to your kids. If they're in an unfamiliar area of a city, they may feel that there's nowhere to turn. In situations such as this, they

---

*It doesn't matter what color, race or creed they are, most people have no intention of harming them. A good sense of peopleproofing will provide your youngsters with confidence and the ability to relax and appreciate their time on the street more than ever.

must realize that there are just as many good people here as there are down the block from where they live. As a result, they should use the same criteria for deciding where to seek help.

5
STREETPROOFING AND THE SUPERVISED ACTIVITY

As parents, we usually assume that once we've dropped our children off at a day camp, nursery school or supervised skating rink, they're safe for the few hours they'll be there. We believe that the staff is competent and qualified for the positions they hold and that our children will be well taken care of. But is that true?

DAYCARE

In the case of infant or baby daycare, your child is too young to do very much to help or protect himself. You have to do it for him. We recommend that you attend the facility as an observer and walk every square inch of its property. Some daycare groups insist on it, but many don't. We also recommend that you make a surprise visit or two just to ensure that what you saw on your scheduled visit is in fact the way the facility is run on a day-to-day basis.

In conjunction with your inspection of the physical facility, check out the staff and their qualifications. When we speak of checking out the staff, we mean the staff that actually interacts with the children. Check their training credentials and job experience. Don't be afraid to question them. After all, it's your child and you have the right to assure yourself that he will be well and safely taken care of.

Talk to the dietitian; find out if she's qualified. Find out what medical assistance is on site and what procedures are followed in the case of emergency.

Don't be satisfied with just talking to the director of the center. Remember the director is part administrator, part public relations director and part salesperson. We found in our investigations that all too often people went to see the director, had a quick tour, and decided. They just didn't take enough time to examine the facility or speak to its staff. All too often we heard, "Oh, you'd just love Mrs., Ms. or Mr. So-and-So. They're just great." Well, they very well may be, but what do they know about safety, nutrition, and child care? It's not that a daycare center, whether public or private, can't have a great director as well as an efficient staff, but it's your responsibility to find out.

NURSERY SCHOOLS

The same holds true for nursery schools. Indeed, the dangers are greater because four- and five-year-olds are more mobile. The first thing you will want to examine is the fencing around the playground. Is it high enough? Is it in good repair? Is it too easy to climb? Next check the storage sheds. We saw one on which the door was badly splintered. We also discovered one that had a strong return spring to pull it closed, which tripped a dead lock with no inside latch. Don't depend on the licensing authorities as the watchdogs of your child's safety.

You should also check out the toys of the playground. Are they in good repair? Are there protective caps on the handlebars of the tricycles? Are the pull handles of the wagons intact? Are the swings safe? Check it all out; you may be surprised. Another thing you'll want to find out is how many children are in the playground at one time and how many of the supervisory staff are on duty—not on standby, or having coffee, or helping in the kitchen, but how many are on duty in the play area? You may want to drive by and do a head count.

When you view the indoor facilities, be sure you pay special attention to the fire exits. Are there enough? Do they meet not only minimum fire regulations, but your standards as well? Are there sprinklers and extinguishers? When checking out fire safety measures, be sure to ask about the mattresses used for rest or nap periods. See what material they're made of and what they're stuffed with. Are the curtains and blankets flame-retardant? It may seem like a lot of work, but it makes a lot of sense. Your child can't do it, so you have to. Again, check the toys of the indoor facility. Are they in good repair? What are they made of, and are they approved by some regulating authority as childproof? If you're in doubt, take the trade name and check with a safety regulations authority. Don't depend on the nursery's brochure or the toy's advertising. Check it out yourself.

If everything is to your satisfaction so far, have a look at the washrooms and kitchen. A lot can be learned about a facility by what condition these areas are in. If there is the slightest hesitancy on the part of the tour guide about letting you see any area, be suspicious. There is no reason on earth why you could not inspect anything you want, and that includes the often forgotten basement and food storage lockers. It's a lot like buying a used car: it may look good, but you can't really tell until you've had it checked out on the inside.

We strongly recommend that both parents go to see the facility at the same time. That way, one can do the looking while the other does the questioning. Remember that when you're choosing a daycare center or nursery school, you're making a decision that affects your child's welfare and safety. So when you go for the interview, remember who is interviewing whom. Whatever they think of you, it's what you think of them and the facility that counts.

SCHOOL EXCURSIONS

As your children grow older and move up in school, the school excursion will become more and more a part of their lives. They will pile into buses and be off for visits to provincial or state capitals, music competitions, or sporting events, and they'll be hitting the street under the supervision of teachers and volunteers. For most of these trips, the supervisor/child ratio is awful. Imagine, if you will, one supervisor to five or more children in a strange city or location. At best, that's five-to-one odds against your child's having any real supervision at all. So everything you can do to improve your children's self-sufficiency will greatly improve their odds.

The first thing you should do when an excursion is announced is sit down and discuss it with your child. Where are they going, who is in charge, and how long will they be away? That's the easy stuff; most of the information will probably be included in a notice or letter that your child will bring home from school. But don't assume that because it's a school-sponsored excursion it's immune from mishap or understaffing. In the southern midwest, a grade-ten class of thirty-seven children were on an excursion to a larger city. The youngsters were accompanied by two teachers. At the end of the day's excursion, a roll call was made and all thirty-seven youngsters were accounted for. The bus pulled out and started back on the seventy-five-mile return trip. At nine-thirty one of the teachers received a phone call at his home. A girl was missing. She was found two days later, back in the city, raped and beaten, alive but critically ill from exposure and her ordeal. What happened? How could a child not be missed? After all, there had been a roll call. What happened was that, first, the teachers had spent the afternoon in a bar and the roll call was slipshod. Second, a boy answered for the girl as a joke. Third, almost everyone slept on the way back and went directly home at eight-thirty, when the bus dropped the children off at the school. There was no head count or roll call at the end of the trip. Quite obviously, the trip was badly planned, poorly organized, and irresponsibly run. This kind of tragedy does not befall every school trip, but incidents that could end in tragedy occur every day somewhere in the country. As often as not it's good luck, not good organization, that prevents misfortune. So when your child comes home and informs you of a school excursion, take some streetproofing precautions.

First, find out how many staff or volunteers will be used on the trip. Then give your child some very specific instructions as to what to do in an emergency. We fully discuss these procedures later in the book. Then check things like weather and road conditions. If it's a trip of some distance, what kind of bus will be used? Is it a bus designed for highway travel? Or is it the standard yellow school bus, which is definitely not designed for long trips or high-speed highway travel? All these things can come into play and directly affect your child's safety.

A school ski excursion ended in death and injury because no one questioned the conditions. The weather and roads were not good; the resort that the youngsters were originally to go to was closed because of poor conditions, so an alternate location was chosen without informing the parents. Two buses were used, and no one, supervisors included, knew who was on what bus. When tragedy struck, parents had to wait many agonizing hours to find out if their child was alive or dead. We know parents who had a child on that bus, and we know what they went through. We are not saying that your children should not go on school excursions—ours do and they enjoy them—but they are checked out before we give our consent, and we strongly advise that you do the same.

ORGANIZED SPORTS

Sports activities are another area where supervision and conditions must be checked. Whatever your opinions on your child's participation in sports, we think you should know that the trip to and from the arena or playing field may be the safest part of the exercise. Not long ago we had the opportunity to observe a large variety of organized sports at all age levels. We were shocked at what we saw. Coaches brutalized young seven- and eight-year-old hockey players. We heard an assistant coach tell a young football player how to take a quarterback out of the game. We also heard a sailing coach tell a ten-year-old that he should take up figure skating because he was too chicken to win a sailboat race. Don't think for one minute that girls are exempt from this treatment. One little skater of about twelve was told to go and stuff some Kleenex down her front because she looked like a plucked chicken with goosebumps. This was said in front of her peers, male and female, as well as adults. We saw the coach of a young field hockey player, who was obviously stick-shy, smack the girl with a stick on her bare leg just to prove it wouldn't hurt. The resulting swelling did nothing to convince the girl that the coach's theory was sound.

What can you do to prevent it? How can you "sport-proof"—or better still "coachproof"—your child? First of all, examine why your child is involved. Whose idea was it, yours, their friends', or theirs? Are they there to participate or to win? To prove something to themselves or to you? There is nothing wrong with winning and there's nothing wrong with wanting to prove something to themselves or, under the right circumstances, to you. I spend time at motorcycle tracks encouraging my youngest boy to do his best, to give one more ounce of effort. But when he says enough, that's enough. Or when I think he's pushing too hard, I say enough and we go home to race another day. It's the same with my oldest; he races supercarts and rally cars. He goes for the win as much for me as he does for himself. I constantly have to remind him that taking him home with his body intact is more precious to me than any trophy he could win.

Teach your children that they are the ones who ultimately make the decision as to how far to push themselves and how much they will take from a coach. We saw a hockey coach put his stick between an eight-year-old player's legs and purposely dump the child on the ice with some force. We talked to the lad after the incident and asked him what he thought about it. His only comment was, "I want to be good and I have a bad habit of putting my head down. He's only trying to teach me not to do it." Apparently, being dumped didn't bother him. We asked him what his parents thought of this kind of potentially injurious treatment. "I don't tell them. My dad says if you're going to play, you're going to pay." Did the treatment really not bother him, or was he just trying to live up to some perceived parental expectations? We'll never know, but you can know how your child feels by being there when it happens and talking to him about it. The best way you can streetproof, sportproof, or coachproof your child is to involve him in the decision-making process. Another way is to involve yourself in the sport and with the team or organizing group.

SEMISUPERVISED ACTIVITIES

There is another type of activity, which we call the semi-supervised activity. These include pleasure skating rinks, spectator sporting events, and movie theaters. These places have staff on site but very little, if any, direct supervision. Your child is pretty much on his own, and therefore must be prepared to react to situations independent of adult assistance, at least until he can get someone to come to his aid.

In the case of an ice skating or roller rink, your child should understand that, apart from the people he goes with, he is anonymous. Once he's inside the facility, virtually no one knows he's there. The same holds true for any of the mentioned semisupervised activities. Because of this, you should teach your kids to follow some basic rules of conduct. To start with, your child should understand that whenever he is in a group or crowd of strangers, he is surrounded by a wide variety of temperaments. He has no way of knowing how any one of those strangers will react or to what they will react. It's something that on the surface seems obvious, but have you ever discussed it with your children? Sometimes it's the obvious that goes unnoticed.

With this said, caution your children never to get into an argument with a stranger. Instruct them to walk away. It's not cowardice; it's common sense. They can never know what the individual has in his mind or on his person. Tell them to report the behavior to someone in charge, change seats or avoid the person in any way they can. If they have to leave, so be it; they won't be enjoying themselves anyway. You should tell them that if there's the slightest doubt as to their safety, they should phone to be picked up and then wait for you in a public place.

You should also explain that people under the influence of alcohol can be extremely unpredictable. Unfortunately, at some sporting events the bottle on the hip is almost a tradition. Mix alcohol and team support together and it can cause some very unpleasant situations. Caution your child never to be a peacemaker; staff and police are usually present to take on that role. If your youngsters find themselves sitting in front of people who are being abusive, advise them never to use foul or abusive language back. It will only add fuel to the situation and serve no useful purpose.

All these suggestions apply doubly to the rock concert. The presence of drugs adds one more dangerous element of unpredictability to what in many cases is already a frenzied atmosphere.

Movie Theaters

We should briefly mention the movie theater. Because of the darkened environment, it can be a place where unpleasantness can occur in the form of sexual advances. These advances can be made to boys as well as girls, and your children should be aware of it. First, we recommend that younger children never be allowed to go to a movie, even a matinee, alone. A child sitting alone is the first target of a person intent on some covert sexual advance. You should teach your children to move if the theater is half empty and someone comes and sits down beside them. Let them know that most people prefer to sit with as much space around them as possible. They should also report any advance to an usher or manager as soon as it happens. Inform them that if they are afraid to move, and it can happen, they should scream. It's better to be a little embarrassed than to be sexually harassed.

Should this happen to your child, whether the individual is caught or not, your child should be picked up by you and reassured that it was in no way his fault that the advance was made. Do not overreact or panic. Deal with the situation openly and calmly. Much of what your child will feel about the situation will be a reflection of how he perceives your feelings.

CAMPS

When choosing a camp for your child, you will be faced with even more things to do and check out. Because of the very nature of camps, either day or stay-over, the activity level will be higher and more adventuresome. Don't depend on advertising or brochures; they are sales pieces, and it is their sole function to sell the facility. Go to the camp and examine the living quarters, diet plans, recreational areas and programs offered.

But most importantly, check the staff's qualifications. It doesn't take much investigation to discover that in many instances a camp must hire who they can get, rather than the qualified staff they need. Not all camps do this, but many camps will hire a basic qualified staff and supplement it with young, inexperienced girls and boys, some of whom are more interested in who is at the camp across the lake than they are in the children they're supposed to be taking care of. So the question you want answered, assuming all else meets with your approval, relates directly to the staffers. There is a very specific way of asking it. First, ask how many staff members there are. Then ask, of that number, how many are directly involved with the children. This number should not include kitchen, maintenance and administrative staff. Now ask, of the staff directly involved with the children, how many are qualified camp counselors or specialists in recreation. The answer you may get is, "Oh, all our staff is qualified." An answer like that may be pushing the truth. It is possible that the staff is relatively unchanged from the previous year, but who said they were qualified last year? You want to know how many of the staff are professionally engaged in their camp specialty. For example, if the camp offers a canoeing program and the instructor is involved with canoeing year round, then you could assume he or she would be qualified to instruct your child. On the other hand, if the instructor is an English teacher who works at the camp only during the summer, then what qualifies him or her to instruct your child in the handling of a canoe? Further questioning may reveal that the English teacher is the national white-water canoe champion and is more than qualified to instruct your child. The point still remains: you must take the time to check it out.

We hope we have made it clear that a brochure or telephone call won't tell you what you want to know. Even a personal recommendation from other parents is of little use if they have not personally checked out the camp and staff. Even if they have, check it out yourself, as their standards may not be the same as yours—and it's the only way you'll ever know.

After you've decided on a camp, your children should be told to exercise their own judgment when it comes to participation in an activity involving some degree of risk. Don't encourage them to opt out just because they don't feel like doing something. But they should be encouraged to consider their own safety. If the scheduled activity is an overnight canoe trip across open water and the weather is not good, they should know they can call you to check whether participating in the activity is sensible. Not long ago, a group of boys from a school were involved in just such a situation. The weather was questionable, the ability of the instructors was questionable, and the reputation of the lake notorious. It ended in tragedy. Your children's ability to make a "go" or "no go" decision will be based on what you tell them before they leave for camp. It will depend on how they will perceive the consequences of such a decision and on peer pressure. The best thing you can do is to tell them you expect them to make such a decision only after careful consideration, and that, after they have made a decision, you will support them and respect their courage for taking a stand.

To help your child evaluate a situation, instruct him on how to weigh the facts. Is there proper safety equipment? Is the equipment he'll be using in good repair? Will he be expected to use the equipment in some manner not yet covered by the instruction? In slang terms, don't let him be a "wimp," but also let him know that just because an adult in authority says "let's go," he doesn't have to follow unquestioningly.

We have only mentioned some of the areas where there is supervision or semisupervision, and we're sure you can add to the list. The same attitude applies to all, though: you can do a lot to protect your children even though you can't see them. It takes your time, your involvement, and, most of all, your love.

6
THE ALTERNATE SHELTER

As soon as your child steps on the street for the first time, he should have a clear concept of the alternate shelter. While the subtle differences between good people and bad people may take some time for a child to learn to recognize, the alternate shelter is generally an easy concept to grasp. Clearly, for a youngster, it's better to say "Avoid pinball parlors; they're bad places" than to say "They've become a well-known hangout for young men who sell illegal drugs."

The alternate shelter, of course, starts at a much more basic level. What rules have you established for your child if he becomes separated from you when you are away from home?

PUBLIC PLACES

Many parents practice the "stay where you are" rule. In essence, it's quite simple. The youngster is instructed to stay at the location where he last remembers seeing you. This idea is all right if the two of you have only wandered apart for a moment. However, if the child stays in a location for over ten minutes and still hasn't been located, then it's important for him to have an alternate plan.

The best idea is to agree on some predetermined meeting location if there's even the slightest danger that the two of you will be split up. Let's face it, there's a real likelihood of this at all large places and events. If you go to a parade, a fair, an exhibition, a science center, or any large show, you should discuss with your child what you'll do in the event you become separated. If you're inclined to forget to make these arrangements, then you should have some general priorities that you know your child will follow.

Most public places have a children's lost and found. On a slow day at the Canadian National Exhibition, the lost children office will process up to one hundred and twenty youngsters. The staff at these locations is trained to comfort the child and to record his or her name and address. Fairs usually have guest relations booths that can direct parents or kids to the lost and found area. In addition, most major events have a remote broadcast by the local radio station. It can also provide an excellent location for reuniting families.

At more loosely structured events such as parades, your rules have to be different. In these cases you may agree to meet at the base of the tallest visible structure. Whatever your method, practice it. "If you and I got separated right now, what would you do?" By going through this pretend exercise, you will gradually develop an understanding of the way in which your child analyzes different situations. This knowledge could prove invaluable to you at a later date.

You should also ensure, before you go to any event or place where you might become separated from your children, that they have identification and that they will be able to tell someone their full name, phone number and address. It will greatly aid anyone seeking to reunite you with your children.

NO ONE HOME

For older children, alternate shelters are important because these children tend to spend less time playing at home than they did a number of years ago. When we were young, it was usually at a friend's house that we congregated every evening to play. The routine was so reliable that most of our parents knew exactly where to call the moment we were late for a meal. "Mrs. Field, could you please send my son home?"

Today, because it's quite common for both parents to be working, it's not as likely that there will be someone at home to supervise play after school. Even if one parent is usually home, there may be occasions when a child finds himself locked out. With this in mind, you have to be far more organized about arranging alternate shelters for your children. While our Mrs. Field happily patched up every scrape on every youngster on the block, you may have to split the responsibilities between a number of different people.

For very young kids (up to ten years old) it might be a good idea for a group of parents to arrange for one adult to come home from work early each day in order to supervise play. The homes could rotate—Monday you're at the Johnsons', Tuesday you're at the Kowalskis', and so on. The kids would then be expected to go to the assigned location after school, unless they had some other organized activity. This arrangement would provide the parents at work with the confidence that their children were in good hands.

The most important thing is to agree on a preset routine that your children will adhere to. The kids who run into problems are generally the ones who have nowhere to go and end up hanging around the street corner or the plaza.

Many schools now have after-school programs to care for children from the end of the day until six o'clock or so. If such a program is not available or if your children's ages or the circumstances of the neighborhood make this impossible, then you should try to ensure that the hours between school and supper are filled. This may be accomplished with sports, hobbies, clubs, the library, or, if the child is older, a part-time job. What the child does should be a function of his or her likes and the family's financial circumstances. But the child must do something.

Block Parents

All your best efforts will not, however, prevent children from being on the street and occasionally needing an alternative shelter. On these occasions the block parent program has proven tremendously successful. Organized on a volunteer basis, adults can submit their names to become approved as block parents. They are then screened by the police department to ensure that they are respectable citizens. On police approval, they are accepted as block parents. They may then, when they wish, display a sign in their window that indicates to children that they are block parents. In areas where block parents are active, the children are taught at school to look for the signs. If they are threatened by an adult, a bully, or an animal, they may then seek shelter in any home where the sign is displayed. The block parents exist to provide emergency service only. If a child is hurt or lost, the block parent will take her name and address and get in touch with the appropriate people.

If there is no such program in your area, you can still recommend neighbors whom your child could contact if he needed help. They need not be parents, just people you trust. If there are a number of houses or apartments that you suggest to your child, make sure to tell your friends that they might be called on. They should know what you'd want them to do in the case of an emergency.

AWAY FROM HOME

By the time most youngsters are into their teens, they have stretched the boundaries of their neighborhood substantially. Block parents, and for that matter neighborhood parents, may not be of any use to them. As a result it is important for you to talk to them about what might be considered a good bet or a bad bet as an alternate shelter. Everybody would agree that a child's first choice should be the police station. Have you ever said to your youngsters that they should go to the police station if they are in trouble? Do you know where the police stations in your town or city are? Have you ever gone into one with your child? Ask your children if they know where the police stations are, and if they don't know, it's time to correct the problem immediately.

Another excellent bet for your children is the fire hall. There is always someone there, and firemen are trained in emergency procedures, should your child require assistance.

Children can also be told to go to the nearest church or synagogue. However, some careful explanation is required here. First of all, churches and synagogues are often quite empty places. As a result, your child should be instructed to look for the office or rectory, which is often located adjacent to the main building.

In larger cities, there are usually hostels run by various religious groups. The Salvation Army is perhaps the best known in North America, and it most certainly represents an ideal alternate shelter. On weekdays, schools are another spot where a child can seek aid. You should explain to your youngsters that it doesn't matter whether or not they ever attended the particular institution; it's a place to rely on for help.

Another institution that you could discuss with your youngster is the hospital. First of all, he should be told to go to the emergency room if an injury requires immediate care. In addition, the hospital can make an excellent alternate shelter, whether the youngster is in his own city or some other city.

Places to Avoid

Children should also be told which places to avoid when seeking help, if you wish, nonalternate shelters. In general, places where there are no people can be considered bad places. In this category, you might find the waterfront, railway tracks, and plazas at nighttime. Judging by the regular appearance of underground parking lots in the crime headlines, we feel that they too should be avoided. Laundry rooms in apartment buildings are another poor place.

In terms of people places that should be avoided, the list is long, and you can add your own particular favorites. Leading the list are pinball parlors. To put these locations in perspective, we'll report a police statement. In some areas of Toronto, when a crime occurs and the suspect is a youth, the police can rely on picking him up at the pinball parlor. Next on the list are public washrooms. Apart from the problems posed by some unfortunate members of the gay element, washrooms generally have only one means of access, and consequently it's possible for a youngster to become trapped. You should take the time to explain to your youngsters the dangers of allowing themselves to become cornered. In a tense situation, they should definitely keep to the open spaces.

Theaters are bad because they're dark, and the noise of the audience and the movie could make it difficult to attract anyone's attention. This is also true of carnivals and fairs. The very atmosphere and energy of these locations make it difficult for a youngster to be heard or noticed if he or she is in real trouble.

Last on our list of bad places is the bus station. Bus stations are generally understaffed and are often a meeting place for some of a city's lowlights. While everybody has traveled on the bus at one time or another without any hesitation, we don't feel the stations represent a good place to look for help.

Less Obvious Shelters

It's worth the effort to suggest some less obvious good places to your kids. Large department stores are reasonably good shelters. They're often equipped with security people and medical aid, and a store clerk can telephone and get help quickly. Another spot your child might consider is one of the well-known franchises. Places such as McDonald's and Kentucky Fried Chicken are known for their community concerns, are open long hours, and would definitely get in touch with the right authorities if your youngster had problems. They also have the advantage of being plentiful and easy to recognize.

If a child is in a plaza and runs into problems, he should head directly for the information booth. These booths are generally located in the center of the action, and the people who man them will know how to get hold of help.

Children should also know about government buildings. A post office is an excellent place to seek help. In addition, most large office buildings have security guards who can help. We're not suggesting that children go into a large complex and start looking for a man in a gray uniform. However, if they were being pursued, they could run into an office and if they couldn't find anyone quickly, they could pull the fire alarm. In a real emergency they should be told to pull the fire alarm on the street. If they do this, they'll find that they have help in a hurry. Sure, it will cause a fuss, but if it's a *real* emergency we think it's worthwhile.

Last but not least, we suggest that a youngster be willing to run into a library. A scream inside a library will get attention in a hurry and they are open most days.

KIDS ON THEIR OWN

The final section of this chapter is less concerned with the emergency situation and more with where youngsters can seek aid if they are traveling away from their own home town. Wherever possible, young people should arrange their lodging before they arrive in a new location. This takes the worry off both you and them. Ideally, if you know someone where they are going, then they can stay with those people. Failing that, your friends might be able to recommend suitable lodgings.

If your child is going to go off alone, and without plans, there are still some tricks which, though obvious to an adult, might be worth mentioning. First of all, practically every location has a phone book. When your child first arrives at a new place he should grab the phone book and look up any services that start with *teen*, *youth*, or *child*. There's a reasonable chance that someone at one of these agencies will be able to recommend a good alternate shelter. Hostels and various other accommodations will be listed in the phone book. Before using up money and time trekking around a strange city, your youngster should be smart enough to phone and find out if accommodations are available and what they cost. Not only will this call provide him with shelter, or for that matter help, but in big cities he can telephone the transit department for instructions on how to find the shelter.

It's amazing how otherwise bright and well-educated kids never think of the telephone book as a means of finding an alternate shelter. It's something you should tell them about.

The other traveling rule of thumb you might offer is that if it sounds too good to be true, then it probably is. Kids on the road often look for the quick gain. If someone offers to put them up for free, they're inclined to take it. You should recommend that your youngsters always take shelter they can pay for. It doesn't matter if they're paying a lot, but it should be a place that has a door with a lock. When young people are traveling, they are usually plugged into a tremendous grapevine.

This information system is created by other young people

going in the opposite direction, kids who have been where your youngster is going. If he's smart, he'll ask everyone he can about the alternate shelters that are on his route. When checking with people, he should always consider the source—do I trust what this person says? However, if a number of quite different youngsters recommend a spot as a good safe place to stay, then your child can probably assume that he's hit on a good alternate shelter.

If your children are likely to find themselves on the road at night, leave them with some good advice. Their best bet is to find a truck stop, and sit up having hot chocolate or coffee. Truckers will often be able to provide children with useful information on places to go and not to go on their trip. They'll be able to tell your child whether uptown or downtown is the best bet in a particular city. Their advice should be followed, as they spend a great portion of their lives choosing alternate shelters.

7
HITTING THE ROAD

It first became evident that my eldest son had the wander-lust when he was around six or seven. That boy could travel farther and faster than Superman. He just *had* to see what was around the next corner or over the next hill. And he hasn't changed a bit—he and his friends will drive 150 miles at the drop of a hat, leave for Florida if someone happens to mention it, or sign up for a ski week before the one they're on is over.

Between school work, part-time jobs, and going places, I'm really not sure when any of them sleep. The plain fact is he is not unique in our "keep-moving" world. All our children are moving farther afield earlier. The methods vary, from public transport, to cars, to hitchhiking, but they're all hit-ting the road. They start with a tricycle and enter the who-gets-a-car-first race at sixteen.

What do you do? You can't stop it. Adults drive to weekend retreats, travel on business, take vacations in other countries. We're a continent of mobile people, but we probably spend fewer hours educating our children on how to travel safely, either downtown or across the country, than we do washing the dog.

My partner traveled around the world at twenty, and I had been across the country three times by the time I was eighteen, and across an ocean by nineteen. I certainly know from my own experience, and from the hair-raising tales my partner tells, that we lucked out. Not every kid does.

That brings us to streetproofing in the broadest sense. We have to educate our children before they hit the road in order to weigh the odds of traveling safely and smartly in their favor.

START YOUNG

The best time to start is when they're young, the younger the better. But no matter how old they are, it's never too late to start. Long before that tricycle goes out the front door, there are things you can do to get them ready for the road.

Take that afternoon walk with your child in the stroller. We point out birds, dogs, and cats, but we don't take the opportunity to start teaching our children about the street. Stop at a corner, get down to his eye level, and point the street out to him; show him the cars and how fast they go. Play at stopping the stroller at stop signs. If there are traffic lights, point them out. Start teaching that green means go and red means stop.

Another opportunity you have for teaching about the street is when you're traveling in the family car. Don't just buckle them in, turn on the radio and drive. Explain to them what you're doing, why you are driving at the speed limit, why you signal, why you have mirrors. Let them feel you are sharing very important information with them. Try it; you'll find they will respond and start feeding information back to you. You may even improve your own street smarts.

Okay, you've taught them what the street is about. They know where to cross, what traffic lights and stop signs are all about. It's all pretty basic and obvious, but now comes the day when they want to go somewhere and there is no one available to drive them. To them it's simple: "We'll take the bus or the subway." Sooner or later they'll be old enough to use public transportation. You might as well take the time to teach them how to do it properly. It's well worth the peace of mind you will gain, knowing your child is traveling safely and wisely.

TRANSIT SYSTEMS

Here's how it works. Take them on an excursion using the public systems. Point out what stops look like, what the drivers look like; familiarize them with the system and have an adventure at the same time. We have traveled hundreds of miles on public transit in a lot of cities, and one thing shocks us every time. The number of really young children riding the buses and subways is staggering. And what's more, they are anonymous—no one knows they are there. Sure, the youngest ones are going or coming from school and traveling in daylight hours. But just read the paper—daylight is no protection. You have to protect your children with education. You may want to consider a travel sitter for the first few outings. We're not suggesting you hire a bodyguard for your children, just someone to keep an eye on them while they learn how to handle their new independence. Or you may want to limit their first trips to those taken with older friends.

After you have familiarized them with the system, teach them these basic rules. If traveling by bus, always have them tell the driver where they are getting off. Be realistic. You won't get them to tell the same driver every day where their stop is if it's a regular trip for them. But at least get them into the habit of waving or saying hello to the driver. It's one very good way of having their presence noted. After all, you wouldn't consider sending your child on an airplane or a train without letting someone know she was there. Unfortunately, it would probably be safer than it is to travel in our cities today.

It is also wise to have them sit close to the driver. He is their best protection. If conditions don't allow them to sit close to the driver, they should sit or stand by an older woman or with other young people. There is protection in numbers.

Of course, the buddy system is one of the best ways to protect your children, but that is not always possible. What is possible is to teach them safe areas if they are alone or traveling later than expected. If they are traveling by subway, they should try to sit in the same car as the driver or conductor. There they are never alone.

They should stay in lighted areas where people can see them. They should stand close to alarms or wastebins that can be kicked over to make a lot of noise. Police have confirmed that noise is one of the best deterrents anyone can use in the face of an attack.

IDENTIFICATION AND MONEY

Kids should be taught their name, address, and phone number as early as possible. No matter what age your child is, tot to teen, you should see to it that he carries on his person proper I.D. and medical information. Of the dozens of parents we've talked to, 60 percent did not think to check if their children carried any I.D. People seem to think about I.D.'s for their pets before considering them for their children.

Proper I.D. and medical information could save your children's life in an emergency. Whether they carry it on discs to be worn dog-tag fashion or encased in plastic for the pocket doesn't matter. The main thing is to let them know what it's for and how to use it if they have to. We feel it's best to include information such as emergency alternate numbers, blood type, and allergies, along with their name, address, and phone number.

Incidentally, any young person who is traveling should take some basic precautions. She shouldn't go anywhere without adequate money. You should explain the importance of never running funds down to nothing. Identification, and the majority of your youngster's dollars (carried as traveler's cheques), should be kept in a money belt or pouch kept under her clothing next to the skin. In her pockets, she can keep enough cash for the day's activities. This way if she is robbed, or loses her luggage, she is never going to be stranded. If circumstances create a situation where she is going to need more than she expected, she can just go into a washroom and take out what little extra she needs. Of course, a money belt or pouch worn under the arm is not designed to fool every thief. The main purpose is to make it difficult for someone to get the money and also difficult for your child to lose it. When staying at alternate shelters, your youngster should either continue to wear his or her identification and money, or check it at the desk for safekeeping. Hostels are notorious places for kids to lose things. Even nice youngsters will resort to theft to get themselves out of a tight situation. Most hostels have a lock-up system, and you can assure your child that it's much more effective than hiding things in a locked room.

HITCHHIKING

Hitting the road also means the possibility of hitchhiking. Almost everyone we talked to was against the practice, but we've all done it and there is a good chance our children will try it at some time or another. We believe as parents we must stand against it, but we also believe that as part of a total streetproofing package we should accept it and deal with it as a fact of life. We must face up to the reality that children feel they are immortal and that nothing will ever happen to them. Taking risks is one way children learn, and hitchhiking can be seen as an adventure, especially if we allow the issue to be blown out of proportion. So we tread the thin line of not condoning hitchhiking on one side and making sure we educate them on the do's and don't of the practice on the other.

One of the most common reasons given for hitchhiking is "We were stuck." To avoid hearing this explanation, you have to do some preventive educating. Make sure your children don't get "stuck." One way is to make sure they always have bus fare. Not spending money, but bus fare. Check with them and make sure they have it in the back of their wallet or purse. Teach them that it's better to take a cab or bus than to hitch with strangers. It may cost some money, but it's better to have them home safely than taking a chance on riding to disaster.

Other ways to prevent children from giving in to the temptation to hitchhike are to know where they're going and with whom, and to set a punishment for hitchhiking and stick to it. Consistency is one of the best gifts you can give your children. They'll know after a very short time that you mean what you say, and they can prejudge situations before they have to test them.

Rules for the Road

Okay, what if you believe they're going to give hitchhiking a try, or you feel it's not the risky proposition we think it is? Well, here are some rules of the road, for the city or the country.

First of all, if hitchhiking is to be done at all, it should be done in pairs. If a sticky situation arises, two minds, and two bodies, are stronger than one. Girls are particularly vulnerable when hitchhiking. Boys also place themselves in jeopardy when they get into a stranger's vehicle, but the media tell us every day of young girls being raped, brutally molested or killed while hitchhiking. A girl is better off hitching with a boy than with another girl. Impress on your youngsters that they should *not* trust the traffic. They should wear bright clothing, never hitch at dusk or at night, and always stay well back from the roadway. Even when they are walking near the road or highway, they shouldn't take their eyes off the oncoming traffic.

You should also make them aware of the accidents they might cause by flagging down cars. With this in mind, they should hitch only in areas where traffic is stopped or traveling slowly, such as on the entry ramps onto highways.

Those are basic do's and don't's of getting a ride. Once someone has stopped, they shouldn't relax with joy and jump in. They should walk up to the vehicle, open the door and ask the driver where he is going. If he provides a vague answer or isn't going in the right direction, they should politely refuse to ride. A hesitation could be an indicator that the driver has more in mind than helping a traveler. If he's going the right way but will turn off at a place where they can't hitch, they shouldn't get in either.

Warn them never to enter a van or enclosed, windowless vehicle. This is not to put down van owners. It's just not a smart move to get into a vehicle in which they would be out of the view of people. They should also refuse a ride if they are asked to sit between two other people. They will have no access to doors or windows if wedged between two strangers. In fact, it's not smart to accept a ride where they would be expected to sit in the back seat of a two-door vehicle. Again, they would be trapped with no hope of escape should the need arise.

One rule is aimed directly at the girls. Never accept a ride in what is commonly referred to as a pimp-mobile, recruiting wagon, or slaveship. That is courting disaster. The police will tell you they're never sure whether missing girls have run away or been abducted.

If you approve of a cross-country or any major hitchhiking trip, make sure the hitchhikers file a flight plan with you and inform you of any changes in that plan they may make on the road. They should understand that it is better to start very early and avoid getting stuck in some remote area for the night. It's also foolhardy to stick with a ride if the driver suggests a short cut. The hitchhikers should make an excuse that they are looking for friends and don't want to leave the main road. In this situation, it's important to get out as soon as possible.

Here is a list of do's and don't's your children should know:

1. Don't flaunt it, males or females.
2. Don't get in a crowded car or vehicle.
3. Don't deviate from your route.
4. Don't hitch at night.
5. Don't hitch alone.

1. Do let people know your plans.
2. Do stay on main roads.
3. Do check in.
4. Do let the driver know you're expected by someone.
5. Do keep the conversation general and your plans to yourself.

Hitchhiking is a bad practice and should be avoided, but if you feel your child may try it, make sure he has the facts and the education that will at least give him better odds against harm.

CARPROOFING

We want to make it perfectly clear that streetproofing is not a single action. It is a combination of your time and your willingness to invest it in educating your children as to the many hazards of modern life. And one of the realities of that life is the growing accessibility of automobiles to our young. Carproofing your child is one of the most difficult tasks you'll ever face. If you're like most parents, you wish that it would just go away. The thought of combining a youngster who considers that he is immortal with one of the major causes of death in North America is not a pleasant one. And yet the automobile is so tightly woven into the fabric of our lives that you can't ignore it.

To tackle carproofing, you have to view it from your youngster's perspective. Kids know that, with the exception of certain religious ceremonies, a license to drive is one of the most widely accepted symbols of adulthood in our society. Driving a car provides a visible symbol that a child is becoming an adult. Think back to the way you felt the first time you drove around the block on your own. You'd finally made it, right? You were free, and everybody who saw you go past knew it. You're never going to be able to deny that experience to your child. As a matter of fact, if you asked the average sixteen-year-old whether he or she preferred the family or a car, you might see him or her hesitate.

So what are you going to do about it? Movies and television glorify the car. It is a significant part of many programs, and the driving skills displayed tend to provide an atrocious example. Sure, you and I know that it's accomplished by highly paid stunt drivers, but do your children know that? And if they do know that, don't they have the sneaking suspicion that they could probably pull off one or two of the stunts?

Recognizing Dangers

We often neglect to talk to our children about the limitations of the family automobile. It is well worth a trip to a wrecker's to view cars that have been in smashups. There is no better place to illustrate just how fragile the automobile is than in their own graveyards. It might also be useful to sit down with your children and watch the television coverage of the Daytona or Rebel 500 stock car races. Point out to them the extreme modifications that are made to the cars before they are used for racing. They may also be surprised to discover that an expertly prepared racing machine can be put out of a race or be involved in a crash because of a manufacturing flaw in a part. It's a perfect time to explain that mass-produced cars are far from perfect when they come off the production line, and that to trust them at excessive speeds or in tricky maneuvers is foolhardy.

Our children are not only driving more, they're riding more, and at a younger age. While sixteen is the legal age to start driving, there is no age limit on riding. Twelve-, thirteen-, and fourteen-year-olds are catching rides with sixteen-year-old drivers, who, in most cases, are inexperienced and subject to the challenges of the horsepower and peer pressure. Children will take incredible chances to be one of the crowd, whether as a driver or a passenger. Driver education is helping to defuse some of the dangers. But it's only doing half the job; the other half must be done by us, the parents. That other half is passenger education.

What if your child is responsible, but the rest of the gang isn't? If you're like most parents, you'll feel very concerned as your child approaches an age where he or she is driving with other young people. You'll probably spend a reasonable amount of time trying to explain that cars are potentially very dangerous. Though your child will hear you, there's some question whether he or she will really understand. After all, did you listen that closely to your parents? Did you get out of a car that was being driven dangerously? Whether you did or not, you've got to make a deal. If your youngsters are in a car that's being driven badly, they are to get out. It doesn't matter when it is or where it is; you'll be willing to either go and get them or pay for a cab. If getting out of the car means that they'll be home somewhat later, so be it; you don't mind. When you make this deal, you should carefully spell out what you mean by dangerous driving. In summary, of course, it refers to any time where a young person is not driving defensively. However, you can spell out some examples.

If the driver is driving over the speed limit, or accelerating or braking suddenly; if the car is overcrowded; or if the youngster is not always looking where he or she is going; those are potentially dangerous situations. When you set up the deal, don't forget to mention to your child that he or she will be subject to peer pressure on the decision to get out of a vehicle. It may not be an easy thing to do, but in the long run, it will show the gang that your child is an individual who is not willing to turn over the responsibility for her life to someone else.

Your responsibilities don't end with this kind of agreement. You've still got to take the time to watch for the people with whom your child drives. If they don't appear to you to be safe drivers, then your child should be told this and forbidden to go in the car with them. Clearly, you're not going to have the chance to check out every other youngster your child might encounter. However, there's no reason that you can't talk to the parents of your child's peer group and ask them their opinion of the driving habits of various kids. If the adult shows little interest, then his child might be a good bet for closer examination.

In the case of dating, the problem becomes even more complicated. If you have a daughter, there's a good chance that she'll be going on dates in a car. In this situation, you'll want to make sure that you trust the youngster who is driving. You should explain to your daughter that if he has any drinks whatsoever, she should refuse to drive with him and call you. If he respects her, he will follow her wishes. If he doesn't, then he shouldn't be with her. If you have a son, you should have a long talk with him about the responsibility he is accepting by taking his date in the car. He should understand that he has her life in his hands and that the privilege of having the car is dependent on his being adult enough not to abuse it.

We have to educate our children to make some value judgments about being a passenger in a car. Passengers have rights, and drivers should respect them. It makes no difference whether that driver is a neighbor bringing your child to the cottage for the weekend or a young driver giving your child a lift home from a school dance or game.

Positive Action

To make sure our children do not put themselves in needless jeopardy, we have to take positive action. The first step is for you to start driving with genuine concern for your passengers and others on the road. Demonstrate safe driving practices and discuss your priorities with your children. If you make a stupid move, point it out; tell them what the consequences of your move could have been. Don't let your ego get in the way of demonstrating to your children that you have a real concern for their safety.

One of the ways in which responsibility and the car seem to be taught most effectively is through the young driver training courses, which are taught throughout North America. Youngsters who graduate from these courses have lower insurance rates than those who do not, and this would indicate that the courses work.

Another way that you can help carproof your child is by making the license and driving itself a privilege that is earned rather than expected. It comes back to our feelings about parents' rights and children's rights. Kids do not have an inalienable right to have their own car or to borrow yours. Whether they have their own car or not will, of course, be a function of your financial status. However, you should establish a clear set of rules or obligations that must be followed on a continuous basis if they wish to keep up car privileges. You might also expect them to wash the vehicle or fill it with gas if they're going to use it. They will be less likely to misuse the privilege if it represents something that they've had to work for. We also believe that a young person with a car need not have the most powerful vehicle on the block. Most young people will get more pleasure out of an older and perhaps smaller car that they fix up and keep going on their own. Again, it's the principle of earning their adult stripes. If, later on in life, they are very successful and can afford a Cadillac or Mercedes Benz, you'll be a very proud parent.

In our opinion it's much easier to learn to drive a car at sixteen than at thirty. As a result, delaying the day your child gets his or her license is probably not a good idea. However, you must view your youngster in the cold, hard light of day before you give the green light for driving. Sixteen-year-olds vary drastically in their maturity. There are youngsters who reach sixteen and could have been driving for a couple of years, and there are others who might benefit by waiting another six months or a year. You've got to make that decision for your own child.

Driving is, of course, only partly what a car is all about. For most youngsters it's a mobile home where they are free from the disturbances of adults. They can take this mobile home to the lake or to the gravel pit. They can use it for drinking or courting their latest flame. Every adult hopes to eliminate these uses of the car and every adult knows that they occur. What can be done?

Aside from the recommendations that we made above, we believe that adults should make a much greater effort to encourage their youngsters to entertain in their own homes. You may not like your child's choice of friends. You may find the music rather loud, and you may wonder what the heck's been going on in the basement, but it's far better to have them there. Your basement will never flip over at sixty miles per hour. If you have teenagers who are dating, encourage them to come home after the party. Say hello when they come in, and leave them alone. The fact is that if you sit with them from the moment they enter the house, there isn't much chance that they'll come back a second time. Encourage their friends' parents to do the same. Tell your son or daughter that if they want a ride, they can call and you'll meet them down the street if they're embarrassed about you picking them up.

Ask your youngster if he could live with himself should he be responsible for the injury or death of a friend riding in a car that he was driving irresponsibly. Also ask him how he would feel if he himself were maimed or disabled because of someone else's irresponsible behavior. The point is that your children must be made to treat the automobile with cautious respect. They should realize that the car should not be viewed as a form of entertainment but merely as a form of transportation.

Carproofing a young person boils down to ensuring that the young driver in your family has plenty of alternative activities. We believe that there are only three conditions under which the car can be an end on its own: if the car is a hobby, and the youngster is in fact rebuilding a car; or if he or she is really enthusiastic about going on car rallies and belongs to a club that teaches various strategies and techniques; or finally, if your child really wants to race cars, and he or she belongs to an authorized club that is located at a track and provides training.

With these three exceptions, you should make a firm rule that cars are for transportation only. Any child who says he or she is just going out to cruise around should not be allowed to have the car. Quite apart from the waste of time and gasoline, cruising is an invitation to trouble.

BICYCLES

Bicycles, on the other hand, are good for a youngster's health, and they are energy efficient and good fun, providing they're ridden safely. We asked several children and young people riding bicycles why they did not obey traffic laws such as stopping at stop signs or signaling, and their answer was, "It's only a bicycle." Somewhere, someone failed to teach that bicycles are a vehicle first and a toy second.

I had occasion to observe my own young son riding his ten-speed on a roadway. Apparently something was wrong with his gears, for he rode with his head down for two blocks. I counted seven potential mishaps that could have caused serious injury to him. I caught up to him and pulled him over. "Hi, Dad, what's up?" I just looked at him and realized that, at thirteen, he thought he was immortal. He was on his home turf in familiar surroundings, streets he had known all his life; nothing could touch him. All I said to him was, "I hope you'll be out of the hospital in time to enjoy the summer." It might seem as if I was being overly smart and not very constructive, but I wanted his attention and I got it. We walked back over his route and I pointed out the foolish risks he had taken. It's not a matter of just telling our children what to do; we have to take the time to illustrate what we are trying to teach them. If he was going to get the dirt bike he so badly wanted, he was going to have to demonstrate his ability to operate it safely.

I came across an absolutely great method of teaching the "tricycle and bicycle" set about traffic safety in a backyard or school playground. Simply lay out a road network, complete with homemade stop signs, crosswalks, and so on. Have the kids help you make them. Now enlist some young teenagers and other parents to give you a hand to run your own safety clinic. Assign the children riding roles, such as ambulance driver, police, shoppers, and anything else that comes to mind. Have them go about their business within the road network. You can get as elaborate as you wish—the point is to simulate real conditions.

Now, have the teens and parents act as pedestrians, traffic police, shopkeepers and, most importantly, observers and teachers of the do's and don't's of the road. Sound elaborate? Well, you'll be amazed at the results and the amount of fun everyone will have. Sure, it takes some time, but we feel it's worth it. The young ones will learn in a play situation, and the teens and older brothers and sisters will have fundamental traffic safety rules reinforced.

You can do it in your own backyard or as a neighborhood event. Kids introduced to this learning-play activity will often play the game themselves. I should add a note of caution: don't let your chosen police force write too many citations. Be careful the young ones don't find getting tickets fun. If you write citations, there must be a penalty for receiving one, such as being ruled off the road for a time, and if they receive three, they must give up the wheels and become foot traffic. Again, be careful not to assign them a job that is more fun than driving. We made the mistake of making one little boy a traffic officer, and he handed out more tickets to more people in a shorter time than we could believe. Remember, make it fun but make driving a privilege.

We've covered a wide area in this chapter on hitting the road. From tots to teens, the central point is that they're never too young and they're never too old for you to start involving yourself in their physical wellbeing. It's not just up to the police to run safety clinics; create your own.

If you think about the hitchhiking questions . . . if you educate your children in the use of public transit . . . then you will have started to provide your children with the streetproofing that will help them make sound, streetwise decisions.

Don't put your child's safety in the hands of others. Ultimately you know best. Trust yourself and your children will trust you.

8
WHEN A FRIEND GOES ANOTHER WAY

Most people recall the problems they encountered as children when their friends pressured them into doing something they knew they weren't supposed to do. If you went along with the gang, you were usually going against the wishes of your parents; and if you did what your parents wanted, you were thought of as a goody-goody or worse. As a result, you spent quite a bit of time trying to walk a very fine line, or at least jumping back and forth across it at regular intervals.

Kids never escape the problem, and as a result neither do adults. Why do their views differ so much? Experts will provide you with lots of theories, but most of us would agree that it's just part of growing up and separating oneself from the family. It's simply something that parents have to endure. However, if you're going to try to streetproof your children, you're going to want to have influence on this process. After all, it's not so much the street that poses a danger to your youngsters as what they will do on that street, and as your youngsters grow older, their actions will be determined to a progressively larger extent by their peer group.

"I DARE YOU"

The pressure from other kids can be overt, such as the dares that we all remember from our own childhoods. "I dare you to let the air out of those tires." "I dare you to kiss him on the lips." "I dare you to run across the railway trestle." If you think back, you'll remember they usually involved some test, some way of proving yourself worthy of your friends. Sometimes they were silly things such as the kiss on the lips, and sometimes they were as dangerous as risking your life with a train. As a parent, the least you wish to accomplish is to limit your youngster's susceptibility to the potentially hazardous tests of growing up. When we thought back to our own childhoods, we realized that there was no way for anyone to eliminate the challenges that will be presented to their children.

As a result, we decided that the most useful thing that we could do would be to put these challenges into some sort of perspective so that our children would have some expectations of them before they occurred. We asked ourselves, "Why do dares occur?" There are probably lots of sociological and psychological reasons, but we decided to simply analyze them from our perspective as fathers. We could both remember dares that we'd been involved in when we were young, but it had been a long time since either of us could recall taking part in a dare. Maybe this would provide us with a clue. We decided that the reason we didn't participate in the daring process was because we both felt that we'd done enough to prove ourselves, and besides, we didn't want to take a risk. Risk? Well, most of the dares we could remember involved some sort of risk, and neither of us wanted to hurt ourselves or get in trouble. So what did this tell us about kids? Well, it's our opinion that most children haven't had much of an opportunity to prove themselves. As a result, they have to create occasions in which they can build their status. Second, children do not seem to have the same fears as adults; they simply haven't lived long enough to hurt themselves doing something stupid, or to see friends killed in accidents. Most young people believe that they're immortal. In many ways, streetproofing them is an attempt to provide them with at least some sense of their own mortality. There are two ways of doing this, and both involve some parental effort. Don't assume everything's all right because there hasn't been a problem so far. Ask the child if she has ever been given a dare and what she thought about it. See if she can tell you why the other youngster challenged her. The conversation should not be used as an opportunity to ridicule the dare, but to look at it as a very real part of life that your child must face. Ask if the child responded to the dare, and ask whether she perceived any risk involved. By talking about it together, you will cause your child to give it some thought and be better prepared to accept or reject a challenge the next time one comes along.

The other thing that you can do is to tell your children stories, from news items or your own experience, in which a child runs into problems by accepting a dare. By offering examples of some of the tragedies that can occur, you can alert your youngster to potentially risky situations.

In some ways, coping with the overt dare is much easier than trying to help your children deal with the many subtle forms of peer pressure. There are examples of the unhappy consequences of these kinds of pressure all the time. A thirteen-year-old Houston girl "suffered repeated blows to her head during a game called Mohawk. In the game, children choose a victim, then take turns sneaking up and hitting her on the head with their hands." One friend said that "the girl was knocked to the ground so hard that she had to be helped to her feet. She was also kicked in the head by a five-year-old boy who was among a group of smaller children also playing the game." In this situation, it was apparent that no one dared the five-year-old to kick the girl. He was simply influenced by the example of the older children and did not fully understand the rules. From his point of view, both hitting and kicking were examples of being rough, and that's what he perceived the game was about.

In another case, rain and inexperience proved a fatal combination for a fifteen-year-old who fell to his death down a sheer rock face near Calgary, Alberta. Reading about this tragedy, we observed that the friends who were mentioned in the article with him were both several years older than he was. One of them said, talking about the ropes which they'd hung over the edge, "We usually fight over who goes first but it was raining and these cliffs were too steep. We'd only climbed some hills the week before. No one wanted to go, but suddenly Wes grabbed the rope and was over the side. He was pretty brave, and never backed down."

Though the older youths may never have thought about it, it's likely that the younger boy grabbed the rope to prove that he was a worthy partner to his friends. It's possible that, like the young lad who fell off the bridge into the Hudson River in the film *Saturday Night Fever,* he felt that he had to perform twice as well to compensate for his self-perceived inadequacies of age or size. Peer pressure works in subtle ways, and it may not always result in behavior that was wanted by the group leaders.

PEER PRESSURE

Children are caught in a tug-of-war between what everybody's doing and what you'd like them to do. Sometimes the friends who seem to have the most influence are the ones whom parents respect the least. The battle is frightening because when parents think back to their own childhoods, they realize that their parents never believed that they were having the influence they'd hoped for, while we all may have known in our own hearts that we were much more like our parents than they ever imagined. We also knew that, at least until we left home, much of what we did flew in the face of every one of their beliefs. If you assume, as we do, that things haven't changed much, then you might as well accept that you're going to feel that your youngsters are rejecting everything that you're trying to teach them. We hope you'll realize that the only test is whether they make it through childhood to become healthy, happy adults.

The challenge then is to allow peer pressure to win the ultimate battle on *your* child's terms. Since you're not going to win every battle, it's important that you win the ones that are most important to you.

A good example of this is the battle that took place over the length of male hair in the sixties. It was the time of the Beatles, and parents were suddenly faced with sons who looked very much like daughters. Some parents ordered their sons to get their hair cut, and some kids were thrown out of their homes for refusing. Hair became a symbol for a whole generation of young people. In retrospect, the length of hair was simply a changing style which would ultimately affect everyone in society. Though the pendulum has swung back again, it was not that many years after the Beatles that long hair was perfectly acceptable in conservative business establishments. The crisis over long hair had been a wasted issue. Long hair had a very limited effect on whether or not a child became a healthy, happy adult. There's no question that many parents didn't like the looks of it; however, they would have avoided many futile battles if they'd simply made some deals about the way it was kept. "If you're going in a swimming pool, wear a bathing cap." "If you want to keep it long, make sure you keep it clean." By making some reasonable demands and giving way on what amounts to an irrelevant issue, parents would have better preserved their credibility and energy for the more serious problems, such as the accessibility of drugs or the changing sexual more of the times.

Hair isn't the issue today, but today's parents will undoubtedly encounter similar challenges offered by their children's generation. And the problem remains the same: evaluating the significance of the activities of the peer group and deciding whether they're a natural and relatively harmless way of expressing a difference from the parent's generation, or whether the activity can actually affect your child's wellbeing. If it is the former, then the best bet is to place some ground rules under which the activity can occur, even if you're not all that fond of the activity. If it could potentially harm your child, then a different tactic is necessary.

Children should also be informed that adults are very quick to capitalize on perceived trends. Both of us are in the communications business and know only too well how disc jockeys and record, television and movie producers tend to magnify trends for their own gain.

Few of us will forget a whole generation of young people saying "would you believe" because they'd seen Don Adams on the *Get Smart* television series. More recent examples have been provided by kids pretending to Kung Fu each other on the street as a result of having watched David Carradine on TV. No parent is going to be able to stop this kind of pressure, but the smart parent is going to spend some time watching the programs his or her children watch. Only by doing this can you hope to be able to understand what's going to be happening on the street.

The same is true if you're a classical music fan. Take some time and tune in to the radio stations your child listens to. You can bet that what's hip to the disc jockey will be hip to your child. The smart parent will talk about why disc jockeys talk the way they do, why the pace is kept high, and why there can be no dead air.

TEACH RESPONSIBILITY

If you listen carefully to your kids, you should be able to ascertain some of the pressures that they're under. Of course, they won't describe them as pressures but simply as "what everyone's doing." Is it a case of skateboarding to the center of the city, or trying to sneak into restricted movies? If your child tells you about the kinds of activities that he is involved in, don't be too quick to disapprove. Remember the hair! It's amazing, but kids sometimes participate in group activities even though they don't get any pleasure out of them. If this is the case, you've got an opening you can explore. After all, your goal—to make the child independent of you—is the same as that of the peer group. Tell the youngster that he must be his own person and take responsibility for his own actions. If the group is sneaking onto the public transit system, then your child should understand he is to blame, not the group leader.

One of our fathers had a great expression: "If you're willing to accept the consequence of an activity, then go ahead and participate." Many youngsters have no sense of the consequences of their actions. They either don't realize what could happen, or they assume they can't get caught or hurt. With this in mind, it seems reasonable to ask your children if they have ever asked themselves and their friends why they are doing certain things, and if they know what might happen to them as a result. It might help them to put the activity in a clearer light. If your children start to participate in some independent thinking, then they've made a major step toward some independent actions.

When your children are going to take on responsibility for themselves for the first time, it's important that you emphasize the responsibility for what it is. Parents always say "Be responsible," but what does this mean to a youngster who's never had any responsibility? Train yourself, as an adult, to explain fully what you mean. If you want your child to be responsible, then try to think of the consequences if he isn't responsible. Maybe a discussion of these consequences will provide a good takeoff point for your child's understanding of what being in charge is all about.

It's only after you trust your youngster to be responsible that you can say, "Look, I know you're going to go your own way and do your own thing; I just want to make sure that it's *your own way*, and not someone else's. You see, I trust that you'll have thought things out. On the other hand, I have no way of knowing whether your friends understand what they're doing or not."

Another criterion you should encourage your children to apply to their activities is their own ability; they should only engage in activities they can handle. If the group has decided to swim to the island and your child doesn't feel confident of making it, then she should bow out. In situations like this, your child will be able to do it more easily if she has had lots of positive reinforcement at home and has developed a feeling of self-worth.

IDLE HANDS

If you think back to your own childhood, you'll remember that you were most subject to peer pressure when you were bored. If there's nothing better to do, you might as well go along with the gang. Right? One of the more effective ways of streetproofing your child against peer pressure is to keep your child busy.

If the pendulum is swinging toward a return of some of the old values, and there's no question that the police and social workers feel it is, then the most recent generations of children have had too much free time! The solution is to make sure that your children are busy both at home and when they are away from home. Remember the expression "Idle hands are the tools of the devil." Exercise your rights as a parent, and make sure that certain things are done around home before your children are allowed to go out on the street. Such chores can include making the bed, clearing the table, drying the dishes, or taking out the garbage. If a child's time outside seems precious to him, he will make that time count—and hanging around is not making time count.

Along the same line, encourage your children to participate in activities that interest them. Both of our parents genuinely encouraged us to pursue our interests to the limits. Because we both enjoyed sports, we tried out for teams, and when peer pressure got one of us involved with a friend who was making movies in high school, there was nothing but encouragement.

WHEN FRIENDS GO ANOTHER WAY

"Why do friends go another way?" The easiest answer to that is that there are a tremendous number of options in this life, and they preferred a different one from yours. Sometimes friends leave a person who is doing the right thing. One of our sons was with a group who witnessed an accident. He was the only one to stay and provide his name as a witness. The rest were in too much of a hurry to get to their baseball game.

Stealing

Sometimes others do the wrong thing. One of us had a friend in public school who was notorious for stealing chocolate bars from the kiosks at the public transit stations. He had a raincoat with pockets that went right through. He would lean over the counter to look at something with his hands innocently in his pockets. When the cashier wasn't paying close attention, the coat would drift over the candy bars and miraculously several of them would find their way into his inside pocket. There was no question in our minds that what he was doing was wrong. But no one ever criticized his activities. By standing around and watching the activity, and possibly even tasting the chocolate bars, everyone who was with him was giving his implied approval to a clearly illegal activity.

One would hope that one's own children would at least go as far as stating their disapproval and avoiding such a youngster's company. However, they're going to do this only if they're made aware of the consequences of their actions and clearly understand what you'd expect of them.

We've all been in the situation of telling our parents what we think they wanted to hear. Parents who haven't left enough time to talk with their children often force certain answers because it's the quickest way of ending the conversation. Unfortunately, this goes totally counter to your efforts toward streetproofing your child. If you're going to understand what kinds of influences are being exerted outside the home, then you've got to provide regular opportunities for talking with your child. Sometimes the conversations will go nowhere. Don't worry about it. Other times you'll be provided with a genuine insight into a world that is substantially different from yours.

Talking to kids about their street situation does not mean viewing the situation as a pal, or from the kid's point of view, but rather presenting your own point of view and your reasons for it. Kids who grow up realizing that their parents have rights and responsibilities will be more understanding and responsive to the decisions parents have to make.

Smoking and Drinking

Sometimes friends go the other way because they're more venturesome. One of us first tried smoking a cigarette behind the school at age eleven. The technique was to practice breathing in and then to put the cigarette in your mouth as quickly as possible in order to inhale properly. The effect was a coughing fit that was so strong that another attempt at smoking wasn't made for two years. On this occasion a group of peers bought several packages of cigarettes. A darkened golf course was the location of this next experiment. The rules here were slightly more complicated. You had to smoke a whole package of cigarettes. The results of this particular experiment were equally dramatic: dizziness, raw throat, and total sickness throughout the next day. So why the participation? Everyone trying the cigarettes knew that parents would disapprove, and after the first attempt we had a fair idea of the physical consequences. However, it seemed adult and if adults did it, there must be something to it.

The first experience with an alcoholic drink, though several years later, was equally ludicrous. In this case the mixture was gin and ginger ale and the results don't need to be described. The point is that if children are inevitably going to try adult activities it might make sense to allow them to do so in the safe and secure home environment. Today, there is a great deal more publicity given to the dangers of smoking and drinking. As a result, children are more likely to be aware of the dangers of both products. However, the fact is that example is a very strong influence. If either parent smokes or drinks, the chances are good that a child is going to want to try both at some stage while they are growing up.

If you've been making a strong effort to keep the lines of communication open, then you might tell your children that if, at a certain stage, they want to see what it feels like to have a smoke or drink, you'd prefer them to do it with you. The chances are good that they won't like either experience a great deal and, in your company, they won't be under any pressure to "finish the bottle in order to be one of the gang."

Drugs

This philosophy does not work, of course, with drugs, which are also subjects of peer pressure. One social worker that we talked to said that all children are going to experiment with marijuana in much the same way as we did with cigarettes. The solution here is obviously not to go out and purchase some so that your child can try it at home. Instead, he suggested parents take the attitude that "the strangers who sell you that stuff are ripping you off, and laughing because they've got your money." In essence, the social worker tells the kids he meets that drugs are against the law and, as a result, those people who are dealing in them are criminals. "You're going to trust a criminal to give you something that you're going to put inside your body?" Having said this, he pointed out to us that parents can't really protect kids from the drug culture. All they can do is hope that their children have enough strong values that they'll be able to place the experience in a context such as "I've tried it and I'm not interested."

Sex

Sex is another difficult area that is as much influenced by peers as by the family. As the police have confirmed, kids are experimenting with sex at an earlier age than most of their parents would ever have imagined. As parents, it is important for us to understand that fact and to appreciate that because they can play the game it doesn't mean they understand the rules. Like most people our age, we learned about sex in the locker room. While we've muddled our way through, we both have a sense that there must be a better way. That better way means taking on the responsibility of talking about the topic with your children.

PARTIES

Peer pressure and parties go hand in hand. At no other time will friends place more pressure on your child to be one of the gang. It is the last place your child will want to be different or stand out from the crowd. At a party, all of his friends will be there to witness his actions or decisions. One thing we should remember is that adults can usually spot the opportune time to discreetly leave a party; everyone has done it from time to time. But youngsters may not be quite as socially adept at picking the right moment to exit without a fuss from their friends. They'll be subject to "You're spoiling the party," "You're no fun," or "What a suck!" The pressure to stay is greater, and as a consequence the possibility of getting involved in something they don't agree with is greater. It's not that they're weak or that they don't have minds of their own. It's just that at a party, when the pressure's on, they're very possibly more interested in what their friends think of them than they are concerned with what we as parents think of them.

You can do a lot to help. In the first place, you can understand what they're up against. It's no good telling them that their friends aren't really friends if they give them a hard time just because they want to leave a party or not participate in something they don't think is right. You have to be more positive and give them some concrete suggestions on how to handle certain situations. One thing you should discuss with your child is the reasons they attend parties in the first place. Ostensibly it's to have fun and enjoy themselves, but if they're worried about being caught in an unpleasant situation then they should leave. If your child attends a party unaccompanied by a girlfriend or boyfriend, then it is solely his or her decision to leave. In this situation, let them know that you are perfectly willing to come and pick them up. Assure them that there will be no inquisition, that you are willing to accept their decision to leave as proof enough of their ability to judge a situation and act responsibly.

If, on the other hand, your girl is in the company of a boy and he is reluctant to leave the party, she should ask him if he would drive her home—providing of course that the reason for leaving does not involve alcohol or drugs and her boyfriend's ability to drive is not impaired. You should also caution your daughter to evaluate the boy's mood before she asks for the ride. If he is going to be angry at the inconvenience of driving her home, she is better off to assure him she can get a lift or that she'll take a cab. The last thing she will want to do is get into a car with someone who is emotionally upset.

Should the tables be turned and it's your son who wishes to leave the party and his date doesn't, then he should take some very specific steps to ensure he is not leaving her in the lurch. He should ask her if she minds his speaking to her parents to ensure she has transportation when the party's over. It's a thorny problem and we're not sure there is a pat answer or action, but we feel it is important to discuss it with your children and find out what they think should be done if it happens to them. After all, if the situation is such that one or the other feels they should get out, they should have the option to do so. The best solution we heard was from a sixteen-year-old who said she and her boyfriend always made a pact before they went to a party that if one or the other wanted to leave they both left. But if one or the other wanted to stay, it was OK, and the person who wanted to leave could do so with no hard feelings. Very mature thinking, but whether or not it works we have no way of knowing. At least she seems to have thought of the possibility of the situation occurring. Her single point was that neither she nor her boyfriend liked drugs and that she would not stay anywhere they were being used. Her boyfriend, on the other hand, was sometimes opposed while at other times he didn't seem to care if they were present or not. She told us that it was very hard to predict when drugs or alcohol would show up at a party and she saw no reason to avoid all parties just because they might show up.

We feel strongly that if your children are showing good judgment they should not be penalized for it. No one knows what any party holds until they're actually there, so don't ground your children or forbid them to attend parties just because they came home early from one.

As your children get older, they will be spending more and more time with their friends. As they reach adolescence they're going to be using up boundless energy, and some of their time will be spent taking some very real chances. Teenagers are experiencing a shift in allegiance away from the family and toward the street. You couldn't and wouldn't prevent it, so what you've got to do is attempt to control it.

One of us has a son who races motorcycles. Talking about it frightens both of us, and yet Father is an important part of the "pit crew." The point is that if you recognize that your adolescent is going to take risks, then you can at least try to provide a controlled setting for this to occur. Whether or not you think that motocross is a controlled setting, it's organized, and far better than the youngster racing through the hills on his own.

If you think back, you'll remember that some of the kids who were leaders in high school turned out to be the duds of the university. As you grew older you discovered that some of the big men or women on campus bombed out as adults. Life is continually turning somersaults and we all know it. "Don't worry that you don't have as big a following as Mike; your time will come." Everyone's used that line, but has anyone told a successful kid that many of the kids he thinks are losers may turn out to be big winners some day? It's our job to tell him that, to make sure that the downs aren't too low, and to try and ensure that the highs are kept in perspective. It's a tough job but it's what the street's all about.

9
CHILDREN
IN CHARGE

While this book as a whole concerns itself with providing youngsters with rules that will allow them to take charge of their own lives when they are away from you, this chapter concerns itself with situations where children must take some responsibility for the control of others in unstructured situations. Clearly, with formal jobs provided by you or others, the ground rules are carefully identified. What we're concerned with here are situations that are often taken too lightly by adults.

SLEEPING OVER

The first situation of this nature that you might encounter is when your child asks to "sleep over" at someone else's house. When this request is made, you should check it out very carefully. Do the parents where the pajama party is going to take place know about it? Assuming that the parents really have given their approval, you'll want to make sure that they'll also be in the home. If they're not, we suggest that your child shouldn't be either. The next consideration is, do you share the same philosophy of bringing up children as they do? If you haven't had a chance to talk with the parents, or don't have friends who know them well, you may ask your child not to attend. Certainly a mild difference doesn't matter, and the significance dissipates with the age of your child. However, if you know them and their beliefs are radically different from yours and your child is still quite young, you may wish to bow out.

The next question you should direct at your youngster is: what other children are going to be there? If you feel that there will be too many for the family to handle, then you may wish to take a pass. If there are a reasonable number but you feel that one of the children is definitely a bad egg, then again, you may wish to reconsider. In this case, you should simply postpone the sleep-over to a later occasion. The next consideration will be the activities in which your child expects to participate on the next day. If they are strenuous or important in terms of school work, the sleep-over should be postponed.

If there's a chance that an argument or problem might cause your child to leave the sleep-over, then you should be prepared to pick her up or pay for the cab. We're against having a young child walk even a block after dark.

HIRING A BABYSITTER

Next, we'll talk about hiring a babysitter. What has hiring a babysitter got to do with streetproofing my child, you might ask? Well, it may or may not involve the street, but it most definitely involves the wellbeing of your children. Because you are putting their safety into the hands of another person, we felt this book would be incomplete if we did not include it. In other words, you are bringing the street into your home and into your child's world.

The first major task is to find a sitter whom you can trust. This is no mean feat, as you will quickly discover. It is nothing to have a babysitter cancel out at the very last minute for any one of a dozen reasons. And very often all of your efforts in attempting to select just the right person are thrown out the window and you take what you can get. That is a mistake.

To avoid this, start your search long before you really need anyone. There are always, of course, agencies you can turn to, but our best sitters came from the neighborhood and were found only after a long search that started even before our first child was born.

Before you start your search, establish what type of person you're looking for—age, experience, male or female. Once you know there are several good places to start looking for them. Any group or organization that deals with young people is a great place to get a list of potentially responsible sitters. After all, you're looking for reliable people, and what better people to ask than reliable people? You may even find the same names mentioned by more than one source. The guidance department or teachers at your local high school can probably recommend a responsible person. You can also check with your local church or Girl Guide or Boy Scout groups.

Now start calling your candidates. First, establish if they're interested, and if so, if they would be willing to come for an interview. This is critical. If they are unwilling to come to an interview, you should strike them from your list. After all, you don't want to hire anyone sight unseen. If they are willing, set an appointment that is convenient for both of you and preferably when both mother and father can be there. You may also want to have the child or children present. Let them see and hear what's going on. It will also let you evaluate the sitter's reaction to them.

Make every effort to find out all you can about the people you're interviewing. Some of the questions you should ask them are: are they on any form of medication that could cause them to become drowsy or sleep too deeply to hear the children? Do they smoke? Do they have any disabilities, such as a hearing problem, that could in any way affect their

performance when taking care of your children? Check on
experience; ask for references, especially regarding children
of your child's age group. If your sitter is a teen, try to meet
his or her parents. Remember, this person is a stranger to
you and the more you find out about him or her the less of a
stranger he or she becomes.

LEAVING A BABYSITTER IN CHARGE

When you have found the person you like and, we would
hope, backup people, you might want to have him in on a
day when you'll be in and out a lot. This will give you a
chance to see him at work and generally get to know him
better. However you want to handle it, we recommend hard-
and-fast rules be set down, rules that can be clearly understood by the sitter, the children and yourself. There should
be rules on who can come in when you're out—this should
include your friends as well as theirs. The telephone, often a
source of great entertainment to sitters, should be kept free.
After all, it's the only way you can get in touch with them
should the need arise. Locking-up procedures should be
clearly understood. You should also give the sitter and your
children room boundaries—where they can play and where
they can't play—along with what television programs they
can and cannot watch. Do this in front of your children. Let
them know that the sitter is in charge while you are away. If
they are allowed to play outside before bedtime, set the cur-
few and lights-out time. You set the rules. Don't leave it to
the sitter.

Remember, undefined areas of rules and regulations
make for some very creative fibbing ("Mommy/Daddy always lets me do it"). Keep in mind your sitter is there to
watch and take care of your children, not to talk on the
telephone, wash dishes, iron or do housework. The sitter's

sole responsibility should be to ensure the safety and well-being of your children in your absence.

You will, of course, always want to leave numbers where you can be reached, along with your doctor's and emergency numbers. You should also include numbers of friends or relatives who could assist your sitter should you be too far away or unavailable.

You will have greater peace of mind while you are away if you feel your children are in the care of a person in whom you have complete trust. But while your sitter may be competent and attentive, she may not be imaginative. So plan things for them to do—some games or projects for the days you are away. Again, boredom on your child's part can lead to mischief.

No matter how much you trust your sitter, it is a good idea to take a few other precautions before you leave the house. If there are prescription drugs in your home, make sure they are locked up and out of sight. The same precautions should also apply to firearms and ammunition. In short, any objects that are potentially dangerous should be safely put away under lock and key. Whether we want to believe it or not, the urge to do a little snooping can be overpowering, and no matter how well we've checked out the babysitter, there is always the possibility that her curiosity will overcome better judgment.

If you require a sitter to take your children somewhere away from the home, set out the exact route they are to take. Be sure your children have proper identification as well as instructions on what to do should they become separated from the sitter. This information can be put on a card and tucked into a pocket or purse.

Whatever your babysitting needs may be, bear in mind you will probably want more than one sitter. While an afternoon sitter may only be required to keep an eye on the children while you get something done around the house, he may not be suitable to sit late at night or stay over. You may want to hire someone to walk your children to school for the first couple of days, but that does not mean you would trust him to take your children on a major outing. Fit the sitter to the responsibility.

One last point: don't overburden your sitter. If you hire him, make sure he is responsible only for your children, and avoid the neighborhood leech who wants to go "half's" on your sitter. There are several reasons for this. First, their rules may not be the same as yours, and if your children see your neighbor's kids doing something you don't approve of, it puts your sitter in an untenable position.

Second, even if the rules are the same, you want your sitter's undivided attention when he is sitting with your children. Should an emergency arise, you've compromised your emergency procedures system by adding more elements. There may be different doctors, different backup people, and possibly different locations for you and your neighbor.

We feel generally that if your child is in the care of a sitter, she should not have other children in the house at all, unless you are home and can personally supervise. It may seem hard-nosed, but when you think of the value of the merchandise you're placing in the trust of the sitter, you should give him every opportunity to be one hundred percent attentive. Make the rule and stick to it.

YOUR CHILD AS BABYSITTER

The next time that you will be confronted with a child in charge will be the first time you leave your own child at home alone. When you do this depends on your child and family, but there are a number of specific precautions you can take.

The first time you leave your children alone should be a

test. When you feel your youngster is able to cope alone, give it a trial run. Don't wait until an evening when your hand is forced because you can't get a babysitter. When they're ready, pick an evening and go for a meal at a restaurant not far from your home, or out to visit neighbors. Explain if there's more than one youngster that there's to be no rough-housing, and no friends are to come by. They should also understand that they are not to open the door to anyone. Tell the child where you are going, and leave the phone number so that you can be reached. When you are at the restaurant or neighbor's house, take a break and phone in on a couple of occasions to make sure that everything is all right. Kids will usually tell you that everything's okay, but the first time that they're left alone can be a pretty frightening experience. They'll be very glad you called. Finally, no matter when you said you'd be home—and make sure that you do specify a time—come home at least half an hour earlier. It's a good way of relieving the pressure for both you and your child, and it will provide a clear idea of what kinds of activities were taking place while you were away.

If your child clearly demonstrates to you that he or she is capable of staying at home alone, then you have the first indication of whether that youngster is capable of becoming a babysitter. Staying alone successfully is not, of course, in itself all that is necessary for your youngster to take the responsibility of someone else's child.

As a babysitter your youngster is assuming a tremendous responsibility, not only for his or her own actions, but for the ultimate safety of another human being. In Williamsburg, Kentucky, a four-year-old girl was shot to death by a five-year-old companion while their babysitter was busy changing the diaper of another youngster. Whether or not this tragedy could have been prevented we cannot answer. It's certain, however, that the suffering of the four-year-old's parents, the sitter, and the five-year-old's parents was out of all proportion to the effort that could have gone into preventing such a horror. While we included the story as a particularly dramatic indication of what might occur, there are many minor potential crises that face every sitter on every assignment.

If your child is asked to be a sitter, the very first thing you should do is take some time and give some long, hard thought to whether or not she is mature enough to take on the responsibility. There's no magic age. It's simply a question of asking yourself, would I trust my own child to look after my own baby? If you feel confident that the answer to that question is yes, then your youngster is old enough to sit; but your responsibility doesn't end by saying all right.

You should realize that if your child fails to perform her job effectively, you're going to feel responsible, whether or not the other family considers you so. As a result, it's critically important that you provide your youngster with the information she will require to do the job well. There are, of course, babysitting courses taught by groups such as the Y.M.C.A. However, even if your child has taken one of these, you can provide additional information or reinforcement about what was learned. It's our opinion that people in North America take babysitting far too lightly.

The first time your youngster is going to sit, you should have a talk with the family she will be working for. If you know the family, you can decide whether or not that particular environment is a good spot for a first experience. But it should be on the child's shoulders to ask them when they expect to be in, and how much they pay. Then you can both make a decision whether or not you want your child working that late. An introduction to sitting does not have to be a baptism of fire. You alone can judge whether your child's first experience would be better with a young baby, a two-year-old, or a seven-year-old.

If you don't know the family, you might ask if you could drop around briefly in order that you might evaluate the scene yourself. If the parents do not approve of this, you may wish to reconsider whether or not your child should sit there. As your child gains in sitting experience, he or she should be able to determine whether or not to work in certain homes.

PREPARING YOUR CHILD FOR BABYSITTING

You should then explain some of the ground rules of sitting to your child. While previously in this chapter we listed information that a parent should leave for a sitter, we believe that many, many parents are delinquent about providing it. As a result, you and your youngster should make up a checklist of information that should be obtained before the family goes out.

First on the list is the number at which the family may be reached. If they are at a restaurant or theater, your youngster should have a schedule so that he will know when or where to call. The next thing that he will need to know is the name and number of a neighbor who will be in for the evening and who has been warned that he might expect a call in the event of an emergency. Naturally, it's also important to get the number of the police, the fire department, the nearest hospital, and the child's doctor.

If the child has a routine that should be followed while the parents are away, your youngster should be informed. It's too late to ask after the parents have left. Your youngster should also ask if the child has any allergies or medical problems. Parents may not mention that a child gets asthma, because he or she hasn't had an attack for three months.

Since sitting is often the first job experience that your youngsters have, it gives you a good opportunity to provide them with some of the ground rules of employment. They have a right to know what they are going to be paid per hour for the evening's work. As a matter of fact, they should settle the fee on the phone before they arrive. Your young-sters should have a clear indication of the hours that they'll be asked to work. Parents can't always show up exactly when they said. However, they should be within half an hour of their predicted time of arrival or have phoned with a good excuse. If they call and simply say, "The party's going great guns!" that should be the last evening your child works for that particular family.

Arrive Early

Recommend that your youngster arrive ten or fifteen min-utes before she is expected in order to have extra time before the parents go out. She should use this period to check out schedules and important numbers, and to find out if the house is babyproof. Most parents know what baby/child-proofing the house means. In spite of this, not everyone does something about it. Your youngster should take time to walk very slowly through the house and examine the situa-tion. Children should not be left unattended but if there is more than one child, these precautions should be taken. Is there a dishwasher at floor level? Can it be latched? If it can't, are there any knives or other articles that could prove dangerous to a toddler? If there are, your child should volun-teer to remove them. Are there guns in the house? Silly question? Not for the sitter in Kentucky! If a room like a kitchen seems to be impossible to childproof, possibly your youngster should close it off and make the place out of bounds for the evening. Are there cupboards that a child could open? What's in those cupboards? Is there a danger that the child could pull out a heavy object? Finally, if your child is sitting in an apartment, she should pay particular attention to the windows. Far too often we read about young children falling off apartment balconies and out of apart-ment windows. Usually they have pulled a stool or table over so that they can stand up and look out. It's important for the sitter to make sure that all apartment doors and

windows are securely locked and that the stools are moved
well away. Your youngster may not think of this particular
hazard, and so it's important that you discuss it with her.

Pets

The other area of concern for a sitter should be pets. The
family your child is sitting for may think your youngster is
particularly cautious, but he or she should check out Rover
the family dog and Tom the family cat. The world's most
lovable dogs and cats have both been known on occasion to
maul children. While it's often not their fault, as they may
have been teased during the day, it's worth mentioning
again that your child is the one who'll be responsible. Kids
can often provoke a pet to its limit, and if parents aren't
around to come to the rescue, it may take matters into its
own paws. If your child has the slightest doubt about the
situation, he or she should ask the parents to separate the
pets and children for the evening. The fact is that they'll
both survive the experience. Separation is even more important if the family has exotic pets. Kids should be kept out of
the room housing the piranha fish and the tarantula. You
wonder why this is included? Well, we'll just briefly include
a quote from *The New York Times*. "The death recently of a
seven-month-old Texas infant who was strangled by her
family's pet python illustrates what the Humane Society of
the United States has been trying to impress on consumers
for the last decade: whatever possible pleasures exotic pet
ownership brings, they are far outweighed by its perils."
The article goes on to say that there are numerous examples
of such tragedies in Humane Society files. They include a
pet cougar mauling a four-year-old, a pet wolf savaging a
Maryland boy, and a monkey fatally biting its owner. There
are enough examples to demonstrate the problem. Even if
it's as simple as the risk of a parrot breaking a child's finger, your youngster should keep kids and animals locked
apart!

Know the Child

The other thing your child should do when first at a new house is pay close attention to her young charge. Is the kid a climber or an explorer? Your child can ask the parents if there are any favorite hiding places in the house. Once all this is settled, your youngster should settle down and be with the child until he or she goes to bed. If the parents ask your youngster to do odd jobs around the house, she should refuse. After all, her job is to sit and that's enough responsibility for one evening. It's our belief that your child should not have any visitors while sitting. If she wants to have a friend by, she should clear it with the family first. However, we believe that this practice should be discouraged. Sitting is a form of dry-land lifeguarding. Similar to the counterpart at the lake, there may be long hours of inactivity. However, if a crisis occurs your child will be expected to react instantly.

If your child is sitting, you should probably leave a number where you can be reached. This will provide him with the security of knowing there's an alternate mind to consult if a questionable situation arises. In the event of an emergency, your presence may be very important.

Sleeping on the Job

If the family knows ahead of time that they are going to be very late, they may ask your child to sleep over. We advise against this if your child is inexperienced. However, you should make the decision. When you're weighing the alternatives, ask yourself if your child is a heavy sleeper. If the answer is yes, then you should discourage the idea. A friend once had a sitter who was so sound asleep that he had to break the lock on his front door in order to get into the house. Even with this noise, the sitter did not wake until shaken by the shoulder. She was definitely not the kind of person who could have coped with a late-night emergency. If you feel that your youngster can stay over, then you have a few more responsibilities to spell out.

First of all, he should ask his employers to wake him when they return home. Nobody needs the shock of hearing someone and wondering whether it's one of the family or an intruder. In addition, your youngster and the employers should establish whose responsibility the child is after the parents' return. If your child is to be responsible all night, then he should be rewarded accordingly, and that should be agreed upon ahead of time.

Before going to bed your child should check that all the doors and windows are locked and that the elements in the stove have been turned off. He should also have one last peek at the child before retiring in order to ensure that nothing is amiss.

If your child is not staying over, it is the responsibility of the family to make sure that he gets home safely. If they've offered to drive your youngster home, you should suggest that he make sure that they're capable of driving. Whether parents risk their own lives by drinking and driving is their concern. However, if they risk your child's life it's yours. If he has the slightest doubt about their competence, a cab should be called. While we believe that the family should pay for the cab, you should inform your youngster that if there's the slightest fuss, you'll pay. If the situation ends with a fuss over who's paying the cab, it's probably not the spot for your youngster to be working anyway.

10
SINGLE PARENTS/ WORKING PARENTS

For the single parent, the job of streetproofing is especially hard. That does not mean it cannot be done successfully and effectively, but it does mean that it will take more time and attention. We hope that both single and working parents will read this chapter in its entirety, as the suggestions we make are applicable to both groups. While the family situations may be different, the welfare and waiting hours of your children are not.

SINGLE PARENTS

If you are divorced or separated and are on good speaking terms with your ex, you are not really a single parent. You are separate and apart, but the two of you can and should act as a unit when it comes to the welfare of your child. But it is imperative that your child knows that you're acting as a unit—that whatever one parent says, the other will back up. Both mother and father should be responsible for discipline and its administration, jointly agreeing to the streetproofing process and its implementation. The rules for the street should be exactly the same at Mother's as they are at Father's. Divorced parents, even those on speaking terms, should recognize that children will use situations to their advantage. But if the children know right from the start that your divorce does not provide them with a lever they can exploit, they won't try it very often or with much conviction.

On the other hand, if you and your ex are not on speaking terms, even when it involves your children, you can be considered very much a single parent. You can, however, still streetproof your children, even if you do not have custody of them. Again, it is harder, as your time together is limited, but it can be done and done effectively.

The Parent's Attitude

The first point we should deal with is attitude. As a single parent, you more than anyone else affect your child's attitude. How you affect it will in a large part dictate whether your child attacks the street or approaches it with care and respect. You must make sure your child does not hit the street with a head full of anger, which will fuel recklessness or revenge.

If you and your child have a blow-up, no matter who started it, two minutes before your child steps out that door, tell him you love him and that you care; hug him if he'll let you, but make it clear that just because you disagree, you still care for and respect him. Don't just give in to something you don't want your children to do just because they have displayed anger. Displaying anger will become a bargaining tool for them. Let your child know you love him and are willing to negotiate or listen. Even though you may not get an immediate response, you will have actively defused some of the anger. When the door closes, and your child is alone, he will have an opportunity to think about the situation, and there's a good chance he'll feel better about it.

The children of single parents can often feel very lonely and frustrated by their situation. The same is true of any child who feels that access to his parents is limited. It is especially true of children of single parents who, by the nature of their situation, are forced to do double time, double duty. Since there are only so many hours in a day, you have to maximize your available hours.

On a day-to-day basis, the single-parent family is no different from any other family. All parents should streetproof their children, all parents should be responsible for providing adequate supervision, and all parents should set the rules and stand by them. The big difference is in support. The single parent probably doesn't have the backup systems that the two-parent family has, and in some instances that can cause the single parent to lean on his or her children. Children cannot handle that kind of responsibility, and shouldn't have to, at least not until they are of an age at which they can understand and cope with it.

To avoid this, the single parent must have a life of his or her own and be up front with the children about his or her personal needs for love and companionship. In the two-parent family it can be assumed that love comes from within, that is, Mommy loves Daddy and vice versa. The second the single parent goes outside the family for adult companionship, the children will react. If they are not aware of the parent's needs, the questions that can run through their minds range from "Is Mommy or Daddy abandoning me?" to "Will I be wanted?" This state of mind can cause them some serious difficulties when they're on the street, confused and unsure of your love and their position in your life. This situation does not ever have to occur if, as you streetproof your children, you demonstrate your very deep concern and love for them. You are saying, by being an understanding but firm and consistent parent, that they are wanted and loved. With this open demonstration of your love you can be honest about the things you need. Don't neglect yourself. Devote time to your children, but also recognize your own need for personal time and activities.

The single parent can easily become a martyr to children's needs, and when the parent tries to break away from the martyrdom, trouble can arise. If your child has had you at his beck and call, and all of a sudden you decide you are a person with needs and that part of those expressed needs is some time for yourself, he may be shocked to find you not quite as available as you have been in the past. So make the transition a gradual one. Inform the child that there are going to be some changes, but they don't affect your love for him, and that you'll probably be a better parent if you are able to spend some time doing some of the things an adult likes to do with other adults.

The Child's Needs

It's important to remember your child also needs companionship and interests, so anything you can do to help him will ultimately benefit the family as a whole. There are, of course, many ways to provide companionship and away-from-the-home activity. One is through the big brothers or sisters organizations. Another is by using community facilities to ensure that your children are not on the street when you are out working or pursuing your own interests. Get the brochures and pamphlets that these organizations put out and go over them and together check the facility out. It's a big help if you can find someone in your neighborhood who uses the facility and can arrange to be there at the time when your child is there.

Participation in a facility of this nature may require some traveling. If so, just follow the normal streetproofing techniques. If you are successful in encouraging your child to join, stay involved—become an after-work volunteer or helper just to stay aware of what your child is doing. Sure, it's going to take more of your time, time that's hard to find, but it will give your child a sense of community and belonging. It will minimize those lonely "waiting hours" by turning them into happy, active hours. Your love and attention are the most important things you can give, and by demonstrating your willingness to participate in your children's world, you go a long way in strengthening their self-image and self-worth. Children will do many things, even distasteful things, to feel wanted and worthy of someone's attention.

If you cannot get your child interested in after-school clubs, or if there isn't a facility available, there are some other things you can do. First, you must make it perfectly clear that hanging around at the plaza or lying around watching television is not an acceptable way to pass the time. You'll have to be firm on these points, but it will help if you provide effective and credible alternatives.

A part-time job is a possibility for older children. The aim is not to get them a job for a job's sake but to have them in contact with people you know and trust. That's why we don't recommend a paper route. Paper routes are demanding and can cut into your time together. They can also take children into areas you would rather have them avoid. The kind of odd jobs we recommend are jobs that can be done in the immediate area under some form of supervision, such as lawn cutting, pet walking, shopping for the elderly or infirm. Again, the object is to keep your children in contact with the people you know and trust. We are not suggesting that you isolate them from their peers; we are suggesting that the majority of their time should be accounted for. The real problems come when their friends are going home to dinner or homework and your child is left alone. That's where the odd job can provide activity and companionship and at least marginal supervision.

A word about after-school care. We feel that all children, right up to fifteen, should be responsible to someone. We do not recommend that that person be the parent of one of their friends. In that situation your children will always feel second best and, should they argue, the arrangement becomes unworkable. Find someone independent of your child's peer group, someone who may or may not have children herself, but whose children should be much younger or much older. This kind of arrangement will avoid conflict of behavior rules. We also recommend that your child have only limited and controlled access to your home while you're away. He or she should use the home of the person you have arranged to supervise your child in your absence.

Sometimes we have to face some pretty hard facts. We have to sit down and look at our priorities. If our major priority is our children, then we have to make some tough decisions as to their welfare. If in your neighborhood there are no community facilities or after-school clubs, and no odd-job opportunities, of if you cannot find suitable after-school care, then you should consider moving to a community where these are available. Face the fact: you need back-up, you need support, and your child needs you. You'll be a better, more attentive parent if you have peace of mind and confidence in your child's wellbeing. Put the systems in place, move or locate in a community that answers your family's needs.

WORKING PARENTS

The position of working parents is not that dissimilar from the single parent's with, of course, some very obvious exceptions. The main similarity is the time the children are alone without the direct supervision of a parent. As a result, working parents have to take many of the same precautions as the single parent to ensure their children are not on the street until they arrive home. However, with two salaries coming in, their financial situation may be better than the single parent's, thus offering them more options.

Full-time Sitters

One option is a full-time babysitter or housekeeper. If you, as a working parent, elect in-house child care, you must select that person as carefully as—or more carefully than—you would a person to take cash or keep your books. Inter-

view them, check their references and personal recommendations. Be sure your children understand that person's
role in the family and that they are to obey the sitter as they
would you. A good thing to keep in mind is that your children will treat the sitter the way they see you treat her. As a
result, her authority will be as credible as the respect and
trust you display toward her. So be sure that the person will
be compatible with you and your child before you hire her.
Remember, a child only has to hear you refer to that sitter
as stupid once to completely render that person useless as an
effective authority figure in your home.

Whether the sitter lives in or only comes to your house
during the day, check thoroughly before you decide on one.
When she joins you, remember that you set the standards
for your children; you must set them, and the person you
hire should be required to follow them.

Neighbors

If it's going to be a neighbor who takes care of your child
during the "waiting hours," try to find someone who is sym-
pathetic to your way of thinking and holds the same moral
values. If your family doesn't smoke or drink, you should
look for a neighbor or someone close to your house who holds
the same views. This rule applies to all alternate care,
whether for the child of working parents or the child of the
single parent. Make every effort to match the alternate care
as closely to the child's home environment as possible. Remember, a lot of what your child learns comes from people
they perceive as authority figures.

We also suggest that you allow your child's sitter some
leeway to make some judgements on her own. For example,
if it was raining when you left in the morning and you ruled
the park out of bounds, but in the afternoon the sun came
out, then the sitter should be able to allow your child to go to
the park with friends. This kind of flexibility should be
clearly understood by you and your sitter and should only

include approved areas and people. The reason we suggest this arrangement is that you don't want your children to feel that their lives are so rigidly controlled that even changed circumstances can't bend the rules. If your children come to feel this way, they may make some bad choices out of pure frustration. So set the rules, but allow your sitter some degree of flexibility to operate within them. Remember, streetproofing your children is not intended to handcuff them; it is intended to educate them.

Whatever the arrangements made for child care, it is every bit as important for working parents to provide supervision and alternate shelters for their children as it is for the single parent.

11
INFORMATION CENTRAL

One of the single most important factors in your ability to streetproof your children is knowing where they are at any given time. While your children will always have some time that cannot be accounted for, you can minimize that time by educating your children to be time-accountable. Time accountability does not have to be drudgery. It can be fun and in the long run will give them more flexibility and latitude in planning their own time and activities.

Too often the police hear the parents of a missing child admit at eleven o'clock at night that they have not seen their child since eight o'clock that morning and have no idea where he was going or with whom. It's even more frightening to learn that these parents didn't even report the missing child until he failed to show up for dinner at seven. In other words, they were quite prepared to allow their child to be unaccounted for eleven hours.

Our first reaction to this was to consider it a unique situation—but we found to our dismay it wasn't. It seems that on weekdays kids are expected to be in certain places such as school, sport practices, and so on. But on Saturdays and Sundays they can do as they please, and apparently many parents don't give a damn until it comes to spilling tears of remorse. We don't think there can be anything as frightening for the child or the parents as a lost child, and the longer the child is missing, the more frightening it becomes, and the longer the odds against a safe return. With this in mind, it's just good sense to make your children time-accountable.

THE EFFECTIVE CENTER

The first thing you have to do is organize an information center in your home for the whole family. It's really very simple to do and very effective. Let's examine what an information center is. It is a central place in your home where members of the family leave information pertaining to their day's activities. This information should tell you or your children where any member of the family is at any given time. In this same location, all telephone numbers are kept, all emergency procedures are listed and all appointments are recorded. In other words, whenever any member of the family needs to know where another family member is, they go to the center and there's the information. The information center allows the family to communicate with each other when time and conflicting commitments don't allow for face-to-face meetings. It gives the family flexibility and at the same time demonstrates a concern for each other's wellbeing.

What else can an information center do for you? Well, in the case of an emergency it can cut your reaction time considerably. Because all information is centralized and recorded, there is no scrambling for numbers or addresses. It allows you to respond quickly by following an agreed-upon set of procedures. There is no point in a child wasting time trying to get Mommy if he knows she is between appointments, or if he knows Daddy is expected in ten minutes. In such a situation, the child could leave a message at Mommy's next call and take whatever action the situation calls for, as listed in your emergency procedures.

The center can warn you if someone is overdue; it can provide you with a logical and time-efficient method of locating that person or at least with a starting point from which you can trace his movements.

An information center can provide you with peace of mind. Let's face it, there are times when it's great to see our children go out, to have some time to ourselves, to play the music we want to play, to read a book in silence, or to shave without the assistance of a five-year-old or the interruptions of a fifteen-year-old. Because we know where they're going, how long it will take to get there, and when they'll be back, we can enjoy the calm before the next storm of "Hi, Mom, Dad. I'm home. Is there anything to eat?"

Before we get into the mechanics of the information center, we should touch on what we call the habit factor. Sayings like "Be careful," "Watch what you're doing," or "Don't be late" don't register in a child's mind because they are said to him every day from earliest childhood. It is only when a youngster has some action to perform before going out, such as writing down his planned activities, or having you write them down for him, that he truly starts to understand his responsibility, both to himself and to you, to treat the street with respect. Create a good habit factor—not just a casual request for caution.

Remember: set the rules and stick by them. If your children are late or they don't inform you of a change of plans, come down hard the first time, and it's a good bet there won't be a second time.

To make your information center really effective, teach your children to be aware of time. The earlier they learn to tell the time, the better. Even a two-year-old can be told what the clock says when she gets up in the morning or has lunch, or when *Sesame Street* comes on.

Obviously she can't tell you it's 7:35 A.M. But by the first time she sets foot outside the house alone, she will have an understanding of what an hour or a half hour is. We also recommend that you give your children watches as early as possible. I gave each of my boys pocket watches when they were around five or six. We tied them to their pants with a piece of leather strap and would show them on the clock face when they were supposed to be back. Well, I can tell you in the beginning we went through a number of watches. It was amazing how often my oldest son would come home with a watch that just fell apart before his very eyes. But it was only in the beginning. He soon came to understand that it wasn't a toy and that it had a very real purpose in his life.

We followed the same procedure with our second son, only we added some refinements. We would go on tours and time how long it took to walk to a friend's house, how long it took to drive to the office or a cousin's house. In other words, you teach your children time awareness even though they can't actually tell the time. Once they have an awareness of time, you can start to come to grips with the responsibility of their being where they say they're going to be. This responsibility includes telling you when they arrive and how long they'll be there, as well as when they are setting out for home or changing locations. Quite plainly, they should be taught to check in.

When you first introduce the information center concept, you're going to be asked, "Why do I have to check in?" You're going to hear that they're only going over to Johnny's or Mary's and it's only a ten-minute ride by bicycle. If you start information center training early enough, this question probably won't come up. But if you're introducing the concept to older children, you can be sure it will. So, in the beginning, be sure to take enough time to explain clearly the reasons behind the center and the check-in. Don't spring the concept on them; sit down as a family and discuss it. Explain by example how it can benefit the whole family. For instance, what would they do if they expected you home at five o'clock and you weren't there? Should they have to wait for you for two hours? If they know where you are, they can phone and see if you've left. Now put the shoe on the other foot. Should you have to wait for them? Explain to them that the system gives them the flexibility and freedom to change locations if they want, while at the same time it gives you the peace of knowing where they are.

SETTING UP THE CENTER

Phone

Let's now talk about the mechanics of setting up your information center and where in your home it should be located. Ours is in the kitchen beside the phone. Yours can be in the den or family room. It doesn't matter, provided it is located where the family tends to gather or pass through regularly. It should also be near a phone and in a place where there is room to post messages and list numbers. The telephone is central to the center's efficiency. There is no use in setting up a center in a place apart from the phone, as incoming messages will invariably be forgotten and not posted. So, wherever you put it, put it near the phone.

When you have young children, you should teach them how to use the phone as early as possible. They should not think of it as a toy but as a useful and necessary piece of equipment that will help them if ever the need should arise. Of course the young ones may not be able to read numbers, but they can be taught how to reach the operator and what to say in an emergency.

While the telephone is central to your center, it is only one element of it, especially for the young ones. They must be able to see what their world looks like and how the family operates. The best way to do this is by graphically illustrating it for them.

Map

Take a walking tour of your neighborhood and draw a map of the areas where your child is allowed to play or travel. Mark the locations of your child's friends' houses, their school, parks, the block parents' house if this service is available, and the routes they use to get there. Now go home and, with the aid of a box of colored pencils, draw a large-scale map that can be mounted on the wall. A suggestion here is to first mount the map on a piece of metal so you can use magnetic markers. The side of a fridge serves the same purpose. Now your children can show you exactly where they are going and what route they intend to take. Have them place the marker and show you their route before they leave. You can also mark their friend's telephone number right on the map. We find it is a good idea to mark our office locations and phone numbers on the border of the map. It is, of course, not to scale, but it starts to give them a sense of distance and the time it takes to travel it.

Chalk and Bulletin Board

Along with the map you should mount a chalk and bulletin board. The chalk board lets you leave big, bold messages such as: "ATTENTION ... READ MESSAGE ON THE BULLETIN BOARD." The bulletin board should have a space for every member of the family and should also have all emergency numbers (fire, doctor, hospital, police), along with numbers for your offices, clubs and schools, as well as the makes of your cars and their license numbers. Your bulletin board is the reference book of your information center. We recommend that the whole family use it, not just the children. If they see you using it, it will become more meaningful for them and they will use it because you respect it. Don't let it become a junk paper storage place. It is, however, an extremely useful place to pin newspaper articles or clippings that reinforce streetproofing ideas.

Daytimer

There is one more important element you'll want to add to your information center and that's a daytimer, just like the one at the office. All appointments, club meetings, game practices, and excursions should be written down as soon as they're made. Now you or your spouse may have to do a little probing here just to make sure the planned activity is recorded. Again, the whole family should participate. We don't think it's practical to record the events of a business day, but we do think you should record alternate numbers if you are going to be moving around and not available for long stretches of time. If it's a Saturday and both parents are running errands, you should record when you expect to be returning and the general location where you expect to be.

Years ago, while I was traveling on business, it became necessary for my family to reach me. I had left my license number and the route I'd be following while I was away. At 2:00 P.M. I was pulled over by the Arizona State Police and given a message to call home. I later learned it had taken only two hours to find me and pass the message on. If I had not left the information, my family would not have been able to reach me until I pulled in for the night and phoned home. The point is, you may never need to use the information—and it is our hope that you never will—but if you do, it could be a life saver.

It all may sound complicated, but it's not. It's a telephone, a map, a chalk and bulletin board, and a daytimer.

Optimal Equipment

For your older children you may want to consider the two-phone system, one for them and one for the house. All my life I grew up believing the old myth about girls and telephones. Let me tell you that two teenage boys can tie up a phone longer than a whole Girl Guide troop. If the two-phone system is unacceptable to you, then you should impose time constraints on the use of the telephone. There really isn't any need for an hour conversation with someone they're going to see tomorrow or have just left fifteen minutes ago. If you teach them early in life that the phone is not a toy, you shouldn't run into the problem.

If you're dealing with older children who have had unlimited use of the phone, be sure you explain why you have put time limits on, especially when you're not home or one of the family is out and may want to check in. There is no better excuse for being late, or not telling you they're changing plans, than "I couldn't get through—the line was busy." So the two-phone system may be a better bet when dealing with older children.

Another piece of equipment you may want to consider is a tape machine for your phone. They are great for leaving messages and are obtainable with attachments for receiving messages. We don't suggest that you issue your children call directors, but if you and your spouse have them, they can come in very handy when you're both out and want to check in to find out what your children are doing. They can also be very handy to give to an older child when you're all going out for the day and you want to give him or her instructions as to where to meet you, or if there's the possibility your plans might change. These machines are particularly useful if you do not have an alternate information center. The alternate information center is the number of a relative or close friend that you can leave messages with, or call in the case of an emergency. This does not suggest that you should not set up your own center—it's just a backup for your family.

If you are a highly mobile family and your children are older, you may consider having an answering service to exchange messages. Again, if you opt for the tape machine, alternate number or an answering service, it does not mean you don't need the information center in your home. However, what if you're traveling as a family on a vacation? What can you do to keep an information center working for you while you're away? Well, for one thing, remember how valuable it is to you at home and just modify it for traveling.

THE TRAVELING INFORMATION CENTER

First of all, be sure everyone has all the proper identification we talked about in "Hitting the Road." Second, be sure you leave your travel plans with someone at home. No matter how you're traveling—boat, plane or car—someone should know where you're going.

Hotels

When you arrive at your destination—let's say for this exercise you're traveling to a hotel in another city—the first thing you should do is check out the immediate area around the hotel and decide whether or not your children will be allowed out on their own. Whatever you decide, set very clear boundaries. If unaccompanied travel is only going to be within the hotel itself, then do a tour of the hotel with them before they set out alone. Point out the house phones; show them how they work. Identify hotel staff and warn them not under any circumstances to enter anyone's room. Inform them that they should stay in populated areas and not play on the elevators or in the halls.

That's all pretty obvious stuff, but it bears mentioning. You only have to do a little traveling to recognize that some people don't seem to find it obvious at all.

Now, it's safe to assume that you as parents are going to want to have some time to yourselves, and you can. A lot of modern family-oriented hotels offer babysitting and daycare services. It's something we advise you to ask about before you check in, no matter what the advertising says. Check whether the sitters are on staff, or if they are brought in from the community, and if so, if they are bonded. If there is daycare, personally check out the facility first before you drop your children off. You may even want to take a sitter along with you—we have and it's great.

If you're going to be in the hotel for an extended stay, a local babysitting agency can help you out.

But what about the information center? It's really quite simple—you compile a book of all information pertaining to your children. Include in the book a local doctor's number—this can be obtained from the desk—as well as the closest emergency hospital. It's just a precaution, but it's a good one. You also include exactly where you'll be and the number where you can be reached at what times. Above all, be sure you check in at regular intervals. Most importantly, be sure you inform your children that you're going out. Don't let them wake up to a complete stranger in a strange setting. Your evening could be spoiled by an attack of hysterics. If you feel your children are old enough to stay alone, you might not want them watching certain movies that can be piped into your room by calling the desk. These movies are listed in your room and are very easy to order. A simple call to the desk can stop this.

If your children are staying alone, be sure they understand how the hotel's internal telephone system works and that they are not to open the door to anyone. You may also want to call the desk and ask the house detective or security officer to check the room from time to time to see that it's secured. It will keep your children on their toes and at the same time let someone in authority know there are children in the room. It is also wise to leave a message with the front desk as to where you are going and how you can be reached in an emergency. The age you leave your children alone in a hotel room is a decision you have to make, but bear in mind it's a strange city and all their regular backup systems are not in place. So think it out carefully before you decide. The one piece of advice that we would give to help you make that decision is that any hotel room can become boring very quickly, and boredom can promote unwise actions. So if you feel fourteen is old enough to be left alone, be sure to provide them with things to do.

Visiting Friends

If your child is going away alone to stay with other people, you'll want to make sure they take an information center book with them. You know what should be in it, but there are some other things you should do. First, if at all possible, deliver your children to their destination and check out the surroundings in which they'll be staying. Take, for instance, a city child going to a farm. While it can be a wonderful experience, a farm for a city boy or girl can be fraught with danger. Ask your child's host to accompany you and have him or her give you the grand tour. Set the boundaries and do's and don't's. If you can't deliver your child, ask that your child's host give the tour all the same. It is also smart to provide the child's surrogate parents with all the information pertaining to your child's abilities and deficiencies. You'd be surprised at how many times parents forget to mention to people their child is staying with that the child can't swim, or that he is allergic to certain things. All this information should be thought out and provided to the surrogate parents.

The same holds true for the country child coming to visit you in the city. While your children may be street-smart, it is to your advantage to check out just what your visitor knows about the city before you turn him loose. Again, provide your visitor with an information-center book and, above all, be sure you check in with him from time to time. It's always great to hear from home, even if you're having the time of your life.

We should mention here that your older children should know about the telegram and how to send one. They can be sent collect by charging them to the home number, and the occasion could arise when the telegram could be the quickest, most expedient way your traveling child can reach you. They should also know it's possible to wire for money and that all they have to do is provide you with the name of a bank to which the money can be transferred.

Whatever elements you build into your information center, we feel strongly that it is one very good way to help streetproof your children. It gives them and you flexibility and freedom, while at the same time it provides the family with information about each other's activities and plans. No matter how simple or elaborate it is, it's a positive step toward knowing where your children are.

12
WHAT TO DO IN AN EMERGENCY

Before we can deal with what to do in an emergency, we should examine what an emergency is. Examples would include a lost child or an injured child. It would also be considered an emergency if you were to phone home while your child is under the care of a babysitter and receive no answer. The list goes on to include children who have to cope with injured or lost friends.

However you define an emergency, there are common actions and procedures that you can follow and that you can teach your children to follow, should they find themselves in such a situation.

WHEN YOUR CHILD DOESN'T COME HOME

Let's consider first the lost child. What do you do to recover him in the shortest period of time possible? Your reaction time is critical. In other words, the faster you establish the fact that the child is missing, the greater the chance of finding him quickly. But how do you establish that he is missing and not just dawdling or taking the long way home? If you have an information center in your home, you will check there first to make sure you haven't missed a message or misread one that tells you where he is. If there is no message or you haven't misread one, then immediately phone and check out the last reported place he said he'd be.

You should always act on the premise that it's better to be safe than sorry. If there is the slightest doubt in your mind, stick it out. If you're wrong, there's no harm done. If, God forbid, you're right, then you're already taking positive action to find your child. We suggest you immediately inform your spouse or a close friend and get him or her home to help right away. If you don't have an information center in your home, then you must establish as quickly as possible where your child was last seen. In either situation, you're going to need help, and the sooner you get it the better. Now that your spouse or a friend is on the way, don't just sit back and wait. Who can you get to help right now? Your next-door neighbors are the first people you should enlist, even if you don't know them. Be sure you supply them with a complete description of what the child was wearing, color of eyes and hair, age and height, and any other distinguishing marks or features that could help identify him.

Don't, however, enlist them to search; they have a much more important job to do—to call, on their phone, every one of your child's friends from numbers you'll supply. It's their job to find out when your child was last seen, and if any of his friends have any idea where he might be. They can also ask your child's friends to take a quick look around to see if they can locate your youngster. There is every possibility that the seach will end there, with your wayward child found at a friend's house. However, in the meantime, you should be writing down every piece of information you think could possibly be of use if you have to call in actual searchers. This should include a recent picture, preferably full figure, face to camera. If you don't locate your child through his friends, start your neighbors checking hospitals and police. Remember, stay calm and you'll stay effective. Lose your head and you'll lose time.

Have your neighbors feed information back to you—but not by phone. Have them run it to you, to keep your phone open for incoming calls only. Look the information over carefully. For instance, if you have a report that someone thought your child was going downtown to see a movie, check out the listings in the paper, if you have one, and if not, get one. Now, see if there is a picture that has been talked about—one that he may have mentioned wanting to see. At any rate, use the paper rather than the telephone book for theater numbers; it's faster. Now have a neighbor start calling the theaters and checking them out. Only calm, rational thinking is useful at a time like this.

Calling the Police

If your first efforts fail to yield any useful information, when do you call in the reserves? The police suggest that the younger the child, the earlier you call them. While you're waiting for the investigating officers to arrive, you should enlist your friends and neighbors to start searching the immediate area surrounding their houses. Again, send your telephoning neighbors to make the actual calls for help and have the searchers report back to them. These calls should be made to your child's friends' parents and older teens. A word of caution: don't involve younger children. The last thing you need is two missing children. When your neighbors enlist someone to help, be sure they get the address of the helper so you can start to identify the area where at least a cursory search has taken place. If you don't know all your child's friends—and we think you should—enlist the aid of your child's best friend and have him or her help you make up the list.

It is also important to have a neighbor search your immediate area to be sure you don't forget the obvious. It is hoped that your spouse or a close friend is now on the scene and helping you out.

It's a good idea to have a neighbor or friend act as a runner to check with your callers, pass on new tasks to the telephone crew, and bring back information to you. We would hope that the actions you've taken would have yielded some positive results and the crisis is over. But if they haven't, you're going to have to enlist more help and expand your efforts. Remember, it's important to take action early and equally as important to record that action so that when the police arrive you can bring them up to date quickly. This will help them to bring their resources into the search faster and more effectively.

When the police are on the scene, don't relax your efforts. Send someone to get a map of your area if you don't already have one. The best place to get one is at the local municipal office, or in some cases, even the police station can supply one. If it's night, a gas station would be the place to look first. The point is that even if you have to draw one, do it. On the map, start plotting areas to search and recording the areas already searched. Make your home the search center. Assign areas in teams and work from the center out. The police will eventually take over, but until they do, stay organized. In matters such as this, the police are the professionals and we're the amateurs. However, given the way many of our communities are cutting back on police funds, manpower may be a problem for them, and they may take a little longer to swing into full-scale action. So give them all the help you can.

Other Sources of Help

There are other people who can be of great help to you in your efforts, and you should have one of your helpers search them out. An active or ex-serviceman or woman (police or military) may be better equipped to head up your search operations. If he does not feel he has an expertise in this area, he may well have some ideas on where to locate someone who does. Another group you can enlist to help is your local citizens band radio club. If you don't know how to get in touch with one, all you have to do is find one CBer, and he or she will do the rest. They are an extremely responsive group, especially in an emergency. A CBer knows all the base stations in your district, and as a group they are highly mobile. Their involvement will not only free your searchers for the more effective footsearch, but the CB group can patrol the streets and relay information without tying up the phone. There is also a good chance that a CB club can supply walkie-talkies and mobile communication base equipment. In all, they're an important group to remember.

Other groups you may want to enlist are Boy Scout or Girl Guide troops. In other words, call any group that already has an organization in place and is used to working as a team.

So far, we have considered only a neighborhood search. If the missing child is older, a much wider area must be included. Obviously, it is impossible for you to organize enough people to search such an area on foot—especially since it could include a whole city. But you can alert a lot of people to be on the watch—people who can help the police in their investigative efforts by acting as lookouts as they go about their everyday activities. It's your child who is missing, and no matter what anyone else does, you have the right to enlist all the people you can to help you find the youngster. You have the right to ask any group that is regularly on the street for help. The faster you can put the information out citywide, the greater the possibility of a safe return and a happy ending.

With that in mind, the first groups you should contact, apart from the police, are groups that operate by radio. Besides CBers, taxi companies, large package delivery companies, and a lot of repair people all use radios. Call them, ask for their help, and give them a description. You'd be surprised how many eyes you can put on the street and how fast it can be done.

We hope you never have need of such emergency tactics, but if you do, knowledge and preparation can pay off. So before the need arises, take some precautions. Have maps of your neighborhood in your home. Know your children's friends and where they go. Have your children check in and set their boundaries. Take several minutes and sit down and think about what kind of a person your child is. What might he or she do in a moment of frustration or anger, or if frightened or lost? Children are people; we should at least put the same amount of time and patience into understanding them as we sometimes do into understanding our friends and associates.

WHEN YOUR CHILD GETS LOST AWAY FROM HOME

Now, let's consider another emergency: what if your child is lost or separated from his friends or group away from home? The three situations that immediately came to mind where this could happen are on a camping trip or excursion into the woods, during a visit to a large exhibition, or on a trip to a strange part of your city or another city.

There are a great many excellent books to aid a child lost in the wilds. If this kind of excursion is in your children's plans, we suggest you purchase one of these and go over it with them.

That leaves the fair and the city. The first thing you must do to help your children relocate each other is to set down some ground rules before they venture out. Those ground rules will, it is hoped, prevent a separation from becoming an emergency. The most important thing to provide is a check-in number. One of the fastest ways for two kids to find each other is through you. If they each phone and report their location to you, you can instruct the second one on how to locate the other. The trick is to ask the first one to pick a landmark (street address or ferris wheel) and have him wait for the other to arrive. When the second one calls, give him directions on how to locate the first. Then have them check in to clear the emergency.

If, for some reason, this check-in system cannot be employed, you should plan some backup procedures they can follow. Before they leave, set very specific boundaries for their excursion and help them to pick a meeting point. If they're going to a fair or exhibition and they become separated, they should plan to meet back at the gate or entrance they used when they came in. In a large park, a central location might be preferable. In any case, they should get a park map as soon as they arrive and agree on a point to meet if they become separated.

We've already discussed the importance of making sure your children have identification and extra money tucked away for an emergency. On a major excursion, the need is even greater. The money can be used as cabfare to find the meeting point, or if all else fails, to return home.

WHEN A FRIEND IS INJURED

Another emergency your children could find themselves in when you're not present to take charge is when a friend is injured. Again, what to do if this situation arises in the wilderness is covered in many other books. But what if it happens in the bush or ravine around your home and within the approved areas of play? Apart from the standard first-aid measures that every youngster should be taught (it's a good idea for the whole family to take a course in first aid), there are some positive action procedures children can follow.

Let's use, for our example, a child who has fallen and is unconscious. Again, we are not dealing with paramedical action, but with rescue procedures. Of course, if there are more than two youngsters present, one child should stay, and one should immediately go to the nearest house and bring help. He should then ask to use the phone to call the injured child's parents. He should also call you to let you know what he is involved in. He can then lead the parents or the authorities—whoever arrives first—to the injured child.

A prime example of just how responsive and quick-thinking youngsters can be is illustrated by a situation that occurred in 1978 when four girls aged twelve and eleven saw a young girl on fire running from a garage. They caught the girl and rolled her on the ground to put out the flames. Then one ran to call the fire department, one to call the police, and one to get the girl's parents. The other girl stayed to comfort the burned child. Doctors later stated that the quick action of the four girls not only saved the child's life but minimized the degree of fire damage to her body. The four girls were awarded a Humane Award on February 8, 1979.

The situation is considerably different if your child is alone with an injured friend, especially if the injured friend is unconscious. If she is conscious then your child can take much the same action as described above. If not, then your child must act faster and alone. The first thing she should do is see if her friend is carrying identification. If so, she should place it in plain sight on the injured child's body before she goes for help. She should do this just in case someone comes along and takes action before your child returns with help. Teach your child that it is a waste of time to stand and call for help. The chances of someone's hearing her are slight, or even if they do, it may take them some time to understand that it's a call for help and not just children playing. Sometimes kids are reluctant to leave an injured friend, or alternately, they run all the way home for help. You should teach your children that the best way they can aid an injured friend is to get help as quickly as possible. Don't take for granted that they will stop and think where the closest help is. It is probable that you will be the first person to come to mind and you may be the farthest one away.

Once help has arrived, your child should stay with the injured friend even to the point of going to the hospital with her. She should inform the ambulance attendants that she knows the injured person and can supply information about her. If the police are there, which they probably will be, she should make herself known to them, again to help with vital information.

We found the best way to teach young people emergency procedures is through simulated games. Set up a situation and play "what if?" You will be surprised at how quickly they respond, especially if the whole family participates. Children like to feel they are prepared for action and trusted to act responsibly in an emergency.

WHEN THE BABYSITTER DOESN'T ANSWER

Now, what about the babysitter who doesn't answer the phone? Again, a cool-headed approach is best. This situation will certainly call for rational thinking on your part. Do first things first. Redial your number. If there is still no answer, check with the phone company to be sure the line is operative. If the line is clear, wait a couple of minutes, just to be sure the sitter is not caught in the washroom or is not attending to the normal needs of your child, and just couldn't reach the phone.

If you're at a pay phone, go instead to a phone that you do not need money to operate and that can receive incoming calls. Remember, not all pay phones will accept incoming calls. Go to a manager's phone if you're in a restaurant or theater. Just make sure you can have uninterrupted use of the phone. Demand it if you have to. Now phone one of your neighbors and ask her to check into the situation. Give her the number where you can be reached. Don't leave that number until you've heard from her. If your neighbor reports back that all is well, then there's no harm done. But should there be some sort of emergency, give your neighbor very clear instructions on what to do: call police, ambulance, or whatever. Have her do it, don't do it yourself. Inform her that you're on your way and how long it will take you to return. Have her leave information in the form of a written note or a message with another neighbor, if she is obliged to leave your premises with the police or ambulance. Return home and take charge.

What if the phone is constantly busy? While it probably isn't an emergency, it's certainly cause for concern. It may be your sitter breaking your no-phone-calls rule or it may be that the phone has been knocked off the hook. Either way, you will want it checked into. Clearly you won't enjoy your time away if you can't contact the home front. For your own peace of mind it's smart to have an alternate number, either a neighbor or relative. Call them and correct the situation.

The plain fact is that emergencies can take many forms and most often they are totally unexpected. We have only covered a few examples here but the message is, be prepared.

13
CONCLUSION

Streetproofing your children is as important a part of their preparation for adulthood as is teaching them to read and write. It's something that all parents do to a degree, even though they may not describe it that way. It's something that everyone could do better. As adults, we can get away with being careless at our jobs. Usually it goes unnoticed, and if we are caught, we accept the responsibility. However, if we slip up and are careless with our own children, we're risking a burden few of us could ever accept.

If you've read through this book, the idea of streetproofing is part of your consciousness. That's the first step toward becoming involved. The next step is to do a little thinking about your attitudes toward kids and the street. An example should make this clear.

In Riverton, Wyoming, a ten-year-old boy who was allowed to drive the family pick-up truck lost control and ran over and killed his nine-month-old brother. Apparently, the truck jumped a curb and hit the baby, who was sitting in a nearby stroller. No charges were filed.

Any parent reading this story would recognize the tragedy of the situation. We'll now present another story that occurred in Detroit, Michigan. The picture accompanying the story showed a little boy at the wheel of a vehicle. Above the picture was the line "Nuttin' to it, Ma!" Underneath the picture was the cutline "He's a Mo-town mover and shaker." The story was short. A young lad "got tired of waiting for his sister to get ready for school, so he got the car keys from his mom's purse, climbed into the family sedan and drove off, ramming a school bus, spinning out, and hitting a house. When his pursuing mother asked him what he was doing, the Detroit daredevil calmly replied, 'driving to school.' It'll be a while before Jason goes to school . . . he's just three." This story was presented in the paper as light humor, and when we first read it, we and probably everybody else took it that way. However, the fact is that the two stories we've just quoted are exactly the same. Only a miracle prevented the Detroit "mover and shaker" from killing himself or someone else.

If we don't continually stay on our guard, we might accept that it is the end result that makes the difference. If an event doesn't end in tragedy, it provokes a laugh, and everybody forgets about it. Instead, this example of the "mover and shaker" should be used as an example of a tragedy that almost happened. It wouldn't do any harm to show your youngster the story and determine if she could identify the potentially dangerous consequences.

A parent can't be expected to imagine every crazy thing that a child might do. However, if a respectful attitude toward the street is developed in the home, the danger of events such as this occurring is reduced.

To be effective, streetproofing has to be part of a continuous effort with your child. It's got to remain in your consciousness. As we said earlier, it's not good enough to shout "Be careful" as your child walks out the door. You've got to provide him with rules and a respect for the dangers outside before he goes out. And these have to be presented in terms that he understands, and in terms of his neighborhood. This means that you must get out into the neighborhood yourself. The examples we provided may not apply to your area at all, but that does not detract from the importance of knowing it. If you live on the ocean, there may be a whole set of rules that you must create in order to ocean-proof your child. We feel that you'll know those rules best. However, if you don't mention them to your youngster, they're of no use to anybody.

For too long, parents, and particularly fathers, have said, "Give me a rest." They think that once their children are mobile and out of the front door, they can relax. But that is precisely the wrong time to relax. Parents, and particularly fathers, have to take a great deal more interest in their children on a continuous basis. They can't compartmentalize them as they may be able to compartmentalize their meetings, sports activities, and poker games.

Most parents have very strong feelings about how to bring up and, for that matter, streetproof their children. It's time that they started stating these opinions to the people that count—their children.

No one will feel worse than the person who has known in his heart what the correct action was and yet, through neglect, failed to act. Streetproofing is not a new thing. However, we feel that it's time that it is given the importance it deserves. Only by doing so will we collectively be able to prevent the needless tragedies that occur across the country every day.

If you think it couldn't happen in your family, think again. That will provide you with the motivation to get moving. As fathers, we used to think there was nothing to worry about; now we've changed our minds. Streetproofing will not eliminate the possibility that your children will get into trouble. Like all of us, they will still have to depend on some luck to get safely through to adulthood. However, if you do some effective streetproofing, you can sure improve the odds. Reading a book is easy; it's time to get out and do something!

APPENDIX

Crime statistics in North America paint a grim picture of violence for our children. Though the percentages of child victims may appear relatively small compared to other age groups involved, the actual numbers are staggering, especially if we assume that our young people are immune or "sheltered" from the criminal element in society.

Homicide

In 1976, there were 16,605 homicides in the United States. Of the victims, 13.5 percent (2,252) were nineteen years of age or younger, 5 percent (838) were under fifteen, and 3.7 percent (620) were under ten. (1)

Canadian figures are, of course, much smaller, but the results are similar, if not more distressing. Between 1975 and 1979, there were 3,368 homicides in Canada. Of the victims, 18.9 percent (638) were nineteen or younger, 10.9 percent (370) were under sixteen, and 8.3 percent (279) were under eleven. Almost eight out of ten of the children under eleven years of age were killed in domestic incidents. (2) This introduces a second, and often neglected, type of violence—child abuse.

Child Abuse

Of the almost 8 million arrests made for all offenses in the United States in 1976, more than 58,000 were for offenses made against family or children. (1) Although this book is about keeping your child safe once he is outside your watchful care, a discussion of violence in the home illustrates just how vulnerable children are to abusive treatment by any adult.

An American study found that 84 to 97 percent of all parents use some form of physical punishment on their children. There were nearly 46 million three- to seventeen-year-olds living with their parents in the United States in 1975. Of these, between 3 and 4 million have been kicked, bitten or punched by their parents at some time in their lives, and between 1.4 and 2.3 million have been beaten up. Between 900,000 and 1.8 million American children have had their parents use a gun or a knife on them. (5)

Estimates in Europe place the yearly rate of child abuse at 250,000 cases a year, with 37,500 of these resulting in death or serious, permanent damage. Emilio Viano, in his book on victimology, sums up the situation this way:

> Children have been considered the property of their parents for centuries, and consequently adults have had a free hand to do with their offspring what they pleased. Only recently has our society begun to seriously question where the rights to health, and in some cases, life, begins. It was not until 1875 that our society was forced to recognize the existence of what is now referred to as "the battered child syndrome." At that time, the New York Society for the Prevention of Cruelty to Animals was presented with the case of a little girl, Mary Ellen. She was discovered chained to her bed and suffered from severe malnutrition, as her daily diet consisted of bread and water. After that case was taken to court, the Society for the Prevention of Cruelty to Children was formed. (3)

Sexual Offenses

The incidence of sexual offenses against children is difficult to measure, as there is no central or national recording system. In any case, it is estimated that only about one in three or four of these crimes is reported. (3) The legal charges for sexual offenses against children range from forcible rape to indecent assault and disturbance of the peace, but all involve some type of violent sexual behavior. They are labeled differently only to accommodate the plea-bargaining system in common-law countries. (6)

In the United States in 1972, there were 46,430 criminal acts of forcible rape, and 47,507 other types of sexual abuse. These together represented an increase of 70 percent over 1967. Reports from large cities claim that about 24 percent of all sexual assault victims were children under fourteen years of age. (3)

When the suspected proportion of unreported cases is taken into account, various studies have estimated that 200,000 to 500,000 cases of sexual assault occur on female children between four and fourteen years old (3), and that 336,200 sexual offenses are committed against boys and girls sixteen and younger, each year, nationwide. (6)

Among reported victims, the ratio of girls to boys is 10 or 11 to 1, and the adult is virtually always a male. Reported homosexual offenses are trivial, but may be underestimated, as these are less likely to be reported than heterosexual offenses. (6)

In general, physical force and violence play a minor role in sexual assaults on child victims (4 percent of 333 court cases). Unfortunately, this is because most sex offenses against children are committed by persons they already have a relationship with, such as a family friend, neighbor or teacher, making physical force unnecessary. (3)

Violence in Schools

Even our schools aren't the safe, controlled environments we would like to think they are. In 8,000 public and private schools in the United States, between September 1, 1974, and January 31, 1975, 280,703 reported criminal offenses were committed by and against children. There were only 262 cases of rape, but there were also 26,710 cases of assault and 9,370 cases of weapon use. The vast majority of criminal offenses in schools (73,333) involved robbery, personal theft or burglary. About 48,000 involved drug or alcohol abuse; 12,866, bomb offenses; and 5,623, arson. (4)

Child Criminals

The statistics on delinquency and crimes by various age groups are difficult to interpret because of the great variety of laws and statutes and the different definitions of *juvenile.* However, the following figures give some idea of the kind of trouble that unsupervised children get themselves into in North America.

In the United States in 1976, there were 7,912,348 arrests for all offenses. Of these, 24.9 percent (1,973,254) were people under eighteen years of age, and 8.4 percent (665,781) were juveniles under fifteen. There were 1,787,106 arrests for violent crimes (homicide, rape, assault, robbery, and so on); 41.5 percent of these involved under eighteen's, 16.1 percent, under fifteen's. Of nonviolent crimes (arson, vandalism, weapons charges) only 20.1 percent were charged to people under eighteen, and 6.2 percent to children under fifteen years of age. Thirteen- to seventeen-year-olds were the most frequent offenders in motor vehicle theft, larceny-theft and burglary, and 15- to 19-year-olds in robbery. (1)

In Canada in 1978, 21.2 percent of all property offenses

were charged to juveniles fifteen and under, as well as 7.1 percent of offenses of violence and 6.7 percent of all other crimes. (7) Juveniles were charged for 14.9 percent of all criminal code offenses and 16.6 percent of federal and provincial statutes and municipal bylaws. (7)

In Canada in 1979, about 9 to 10 percent of most crimes were charged to juveniles, including homicide, robbery, sexual offenses, and offensive weapons charges. Juveniles were responsible for about 5 percent of offenses to do with drugs and alcohol. (9) Of the 631 homicides that occurred in Canada in the same year, 19.9 percent of the suspects were nineteen and under, and 3.3 percent were fifteen and under. (2)

Victimology

Victimologists believe that, just as certain persons have a high probability of committing a crime, others have the same likelihood for being a victim of that crime. This means that the victim may in some way actually cause or instigate an assault. (3)

There is a particular group of child victims of sexual offenses who "consent," either intentionally or unwittingly, or offer only passive resistance. The offender infers acquiescence, if not agreement. These are not necessarily maladjusted children. They are simply "submissive, seductive girls ready to participate in any relationship at a superficial level." In past research on sex offenses, female victims were classified as "collaborative" in 7.8 percent of 330 court cases, as "nonobjecting" in 40 percent of 1,994 cases, as "encouraging" in 66 percent of 73 cases, as "fully participating" in 60 percent of 73 cases, and as "seducers" in 185 cases. (3)

REFERENCES

1. "Crime in the United States, 1976." Uniform Crime Reports, issued by Clarence M. Kelley, Federal Bureau of Investigation, Department of Justice, September 28, 1977.

2. "Homicide Statistics, 1979." Statistics Canada: Report 85-209.

3. *Victimology: A New Focus. Volume 14L: Violence and Its Victims.* Conclusions and recommendations adopted by the First International Symposium on Victimology held in Jerusalem, September 2–6, 1973. Israel Drapkin and Emilio Viano, Lexington Books. Toronto.

4. *Sourcebook of Criminal Justice Statistics, 1978.* U.S. Department of Justice, Law Enforcement Assistance Administration, National Criminal Justice Information and Statistics Service. Toronto.

5. "Violence Toward Children in the United States." Richard Gelles, *American Journal of Orthopsychiatry,* 48(4), October 1978, pp. 580–592.

6. "An Estimate of Nationwide Incidence of Sexual Offenses Against Children." Edward Sarafino, *Child Welfare,* Volume LVIII, No. 2, February 1979, pp. 127–134.

7. "Crime and Traffic Enforcement Statistics, 1978." Statistics Canada Report 85-205.

8. "Juvenile Delinquents, 1978." Statistics Canada Report 85-202.

9. "Uniform Crime Report, 1979." Statistics Canada Report 85-205.

A GUIDELINE QUIZ TO STREETPROOFING EFFECTIVELY

When adding up your score, do not count questions that do not apply to your situation. Of the remaining questions only score those to which you can give a positive response. When an answer is in doubt, count as a negative.

	YES	NO
· Does your child know what to do if lost?	—	—
· Have you ever discussed peer pressure with your child?	—	—
· Have you ever discussed with your child what abnormal behavior is?	—	—

	YES	NO
· Have you discussed when your child should get out of a friend's car?	—	—
· Have you discussed with your children what should be done if they find themselves at a questionable party?	—	—
· Have you ever taken a walking tour of your neighborhood?	—	—
· Have you physically checked out the facilities your child attends?	—	—
a) Day care?	—	—
b) Sports?	—	—
c) Social?	—	—
· Does your child know when to reject adult authority?	—	—
· Have you ever discussed emergency procedures with your child?	—	—
· Does your child carry personal identification and medical information?	—	—
· Is your child prompt?	—	—
· Are you prompt?	—	—
· Do you know if your child is a follower?	—	—
· Do you know if your child is a wanderer?	—	—
· Can you account for your child's whereabouts hourly?	—	—
· Have you discussed with your child who might be the best people to approach if he or she needs help?	—	—
· Have you ever done any public transit training with your child?	—	—
· Do you know specifically how much money your child has to spend?	—	—

	YES	NO

· In the presence of your child, do you display a positive attitude toward the police? ___ ___

· Is your home a gathering place for kids? ___ ___
    a) Have you thought of why? ___ ___
    b) Do you know whose house is a gathering place for kids? ___ ___

· Do you know the telephone numbers and addresses of your child's friends? ___ ___

· Have you met the parents of your child's friends? ___ ___

· Do you feel you:
    a) Listen to your child? ___ ___
    b) Spend enough time with your child? ___ ___

· Does your child know how and where to reach you at any time? ___ ___

· Do you know how and where to reach your child at any time? ___ ___

· Do you know the route your child takes to school? ___ ___

· Have you ever walked the route yourself? ___ ___

· In your neighborhood, do you know if there are any:
    a) Abandoned buildings? ___ ___
    b) Vacant lots? ___ ___
    c) Unlighted walkways? ___ ___
    d) Creeks subject to flooding? ___ ___

· Do you know if the police patrol your neighborhood on a regular basis? ___ ___

· Do you know your child's favorite place to play? ___ ___
    a) Have you ever been there? ___ ___
    b) Have you ever asked him where it is? ___ ___

Scoring

100% positive score	Excellent
90–99% positive score	You're doing a good job
80–89% positive score	You're trying
70–79% positive score	You can do better
60–69% positive score	You know what you have to do
59% and below	Start now—it's never too late

ABOUT THE AUTHORS

RICHARD C. GOSSAGE and MELVIN J. GUNTON are partners in an enterprise called Program Design Group. The partnership specializes in preparing written and visual materials for the commercial world. The two authors have written over 100 audio-visual and multi-image scripts, over 50 documentary films, teaching manuals, corporate stories, advertising campaigns, government promotion campaigns, etc. The two authors have, between them, four children. As parents, they have been very concerned by the increasing attacks on children in our streets. The book itself resulted from a tragedy that occurred in Toronto, Canada in the summer of 1980.

SEAL BOOKS

Offers you a list of outstanding fiction, non-fiction and classics of Canadian literature in paperback by Canadian authors, available at all good bookstores throughout Canada.

The Mark of Canadian Bestsellers